Living the Good Life with Autism

by the same author

Discovering My Autism
Apologia Pro Vita Sua (with Apologies to Cardinal Newman)
Edgar Schneider
ISBN 1 85302 724 3

of related interest

Pretending to be Normal
Living with Asperger's Syndrome
Liane Holliday Willey
ISBN 1 85302 749 9

Asperger Syndrome, the Universe and Everything
Kenneth Hall
ISBN 1 85302 930 0

Freaks, Geeks and Asperger Syndrome
A User Guide to Adolescence
Luke Jackson
ISBN 1 84310 098 3

Making Sense of the Unfeasible
My Life Journey with Asperger Syndrome
Marc Fleisher
ISBN 1 84310 165 3

Living the Good Life with Autism

Edgar Schneider

Jessica Kingsley Publishers
London and New York

The right of Edgar Schneider to be identified as author of this work has been asserted by him in accordance with the Copyright, Designs and Patents Act 1988.

First published in the United Kingdom in 2003
by Jessica Kingsley Publishers Ltd
116 Pentonville Road
London N1 9JB, England
and
29 West 35th Street, 10th fl.
New York, NY 10001-2299, USA

www.jkp.com

Library of Congress Cataloging in Publication Data
Schneider, Edgar, 1932-
    Living the good life with autism / Edgar R. Schneider.
        p. cm.
    Includes bibliographical references and index.
    ISBN 1-84310-712-0 (alk paper)
    1. Autism. 2. Asperger's syndrome. 3. Autism--Patients--Family relationships. 4. Asperger's syndrome--Patients--Family relationships. I. Title.

    RC553.A88 S363 2002
    616.89'82'0092--dc21   2002021871

British Library Cataloguing in Publication Data
A CIP catalogue record for this book is available from the British Library

ISBN 1 84310 712 0

Printed and Bound in Great Britain by
Athenaeum Press, Gateshead, Tyne and Wear

To Alexandra, my wife, for her wonderful contributions, to Jasmine Lee O'Neill, for her inspirational book Through the Eyes of Aliens *(which has a theme exactly like this title), and to Elaine Needell, M.D., a fellow music-lover, who graciously acted as my technical advisor.*

Contents

Prologue

I was baptized 'Edgar', so I guess that's what God calls me. My friends usually address me as 'Ed'. To people I don't like, I'm 'Mr Schneider'.

I have Asperger Syndrome. This is the highest-functioning form of autism, but, unlike most autistic people today, who are diagnosed as young children, I only found out in the spring of 1995 as a result of reading an article in *The New Yorker* by Oliver Sacks.[1] Of course, nobody can be faulted for the fact that I discovered this so late in life; that's just the way life goes.

In the year in which autism was first given a name, I graduated from high school. This renders such things as early diagnosis or intervention irrelevant. I attribute my autism to brain damage caused by infectious diseases in early childhood (specifically, it was scarlet fever and pertussis, at about the age of three). All of this is described, in extensive detail, in my published autobiography.[2] I could very likely say that, in the spring of 1995, my life began all over again. At the very least, I was able to view it again, this time with insight instead of bewilderment.

Very likely, the biggest problem with autism is that it is one of the most misunderstood disabilities anywhere, if not the most. As a result, it is often misdiagnosed. Even when correctly diagnosed, it is often for the wrong reasons. In either case, the results are therapies that vary from the inappropriate to the counterproductive.

The situation is improving, albeit slowly. With increased knowledge of autism, more cases are being diagnosed correctly. This may be a reason for the increase in the reported cases of autism, but that is a speculation. A graduate student in special education told me that autism is becoming what he calls the new 'boutique diagnosis'. (Years ago, schizophrenia held that dubious honor.) The need for more knowledge is by no means over. As Alexander Pope said, in his *Essay on Criticism*: 'A little learning is a dang'rous thing; Drink deep or taste not the Pierian spring.'

It has been said, more than once, that the best source of information about autism is autistic people who are able to communicate, one way or another. It was my intention, in my autobiography, to give to the non-autistic, certain insights into this type of personality. One review of my autobiography said that it shows how the world is perceived, and opinions are formed, by the autistic mind. Although I have written two chapters, one giving my view on theological matters and one on political matters, this is not to bring the reader around to my way of thinking about these things, but to show how I arrived at these perceptions. Even if I wanted to try to convince the reader of their truth, I would likely not succeed, since I am not a persuader, but strictly an explainer.

Lest any of this be construed to imply that I do not welcome dissenting viewpoints, I should like to point out that the people who have, over the years, been most valuable to my intellectual development are those who have disagreed with me and have been very specific about their reasons. In some cases, after researching their ideas, they have caused me to change or modify my views or, after much more thorough research, I have come out of it with a much firmer foundation for my point of view.

I should like to point out to the reader how an autistic person, left to his or her own devices, is able to create, within the constraints of reality, a life that is rewarding and fulfilling. One book that deals with this beautifully, though from a different standpoint, is *Through The Eyes Of Aliens.*[3]

Allow me, at this point, to tell a number of things about myself in the hope that this will illustrate that in spite of being 'disabled', I have managed to adapt quite well, and build a rich, full life (and I am far from unique in that regard).

I was born in and grew up in Brooklyn, New York; I attended New York City public schools, and graduated, in 1950, from that city's High School of Music and Art, where I was a member of the Arista Society. This name is from the Greek word for 'best' and these organizations were unique to the city. They have now been superseded by the National Honor Society. In 1954, I graduated in a liberal arts program from City College of New York (BA *cum laude* and Phi Beta Kappa). My graduate study was in physics and mathematics (American University, MA 1970). I am also interested in music, art, literature, languages, history, philosophy, theology, politics, and economics and I am actively involved in many of these. My 'manual' hobbies include photography, gourmet cooking, leathercrafting, and small-bore rifle target shooting. I have included my file of recipes as Appendix A as an example of my gourmet cooking.

I am retired from a major computer company, where I was a mathematician and scientific computer programmer. In June 1999 I married a very creative and talented high-functioning autistic woman, Alexandra. In addition to my published autobiography, I have been a speaker at meetings and workshops concerned with autism.

I have to say however that it has not always been a good life, nor did it get that way overnight and I most certainly cannot compare myself to the goddess Athena, who in Greek mythology was born by springing, in full armor, from the brow of Zeus!

During childhood and early adolescence, my family and teachers were not at all optimistic and as a child, I was looked upon as little more than an anti-social brat. However my rite of passage to adolescence consisted of having this title change to a 'cold fish' and a 'party pooper'. During that time one expression I heard, all too often, was, 'What are we ever going to do with him?'

This is something that is said all too often, even by well-meaning NT people. ('NT' is an abbreviation for 'neurologically typical', a jargon term to describe the non-autistic.) They speak of things like 'that awful affliction', and 'being trapped inside that terrible disability'. I beg to demur. First, it seems as if they see only to the surface and, more importantly, that these conclusions are reached by evaluating the situation according to their own standards. There is a story that I would like to tell that illustrates the problem with this approach.

> A boy scout is walking down a busy street, and he sees an old lady standing on the corner. He says to himself, 'Poor old lady. She wants to cross the street, but is afraid to because of the traffic. I will help her across. That will be my good deed for the day.' He approaches the lady and says, 'Madam, have no fear. I will see that you get across the street safely.' He then took the lady by the arm and escorted her through traffic to the opposite corner. When they got there, he said, 'There you are madam, safe and sound.' The lady said, 'Thank you very much, sonny, but when I was standing on that corner, I was waiting for a bus.'

In all fairness, the autistic are oftentimes hampered, when conveying their vision and their evaluation to the NT, by the inability to communicate, a true disability with which many of them are afflicted.conveying their vision and their evaluation to the NT, by the autistic, is oftentimes hampered by the inability to communicate, a true disability with which many of them are afflicted. NT people, therefore, cannot be faulted, since their perceptions of the autistic stem from ignorance, which is curable by information and understanding. So, I hope to show to NT people that there is much more to this than meets their eyes.

Opinions

Some Reinforced, Some Modified

In the three years since my autobiography was published in 1998, I have had occasion to revisit some of the opinions that I originally stated. They regard both the nature and origins of autism, and the way in which autistic people relate to the world of the non-autistic. I have learned much since then, some things by reading and responding to posts to Internet autism lists, others in the exchange of ideas that took place in talks that I have given to parents and professionals, both locally and elsewhere.

Perhaps a bit of background is in order here. On the Internet, there is a phenomenon called the 'listservice' or 'list', for short. If someone subscribes, then any message posted to the list is automatically forwarded to all subscribers. They are usually dedicated to a subject in which the subscribers share a common interest.

In moving some of those opinions beyond generalities, I have learned many details that have convinced me, as much as is possible, that I was correct. For others, the new information pointed out to me that perhaps, at best, I did not know the whole story. For each of those, whether I was right or wrong, it was a learning experience. As such, even when I had to stand corrected, I saw it as an improvement, because my opinions had moved closer to the truth.

This last remark is far from superficial. It relates to my ideas about the truth and our ability to know it. There is an analogy with the field of specialization that I chose for my graduate study in mathematics: numerical analysis. I should like to explain. Most mathematical problems do not have a closed-form solution, which is one that can be reached in a finite number of computational steps. Thus, methods must be developed to approximate that solution to whatever degree of accuracy one desires. Before one can devise such a method, it must be proven that a solution exists, and then it must also be proven that this method does indeed converge on that solution as the number of steps becomes infinite.

This has philosophical significance for the search for truth. While one may, as I do, believe in the existence of objective truth, the best one can ever do is approximate it. In my view, this is what learning is all about. To claim that truth does not exist, because it cannot be wholly known, is to abandon learning. As to realizing the need to approximate it, even someone such as St. Paul, who dedicated his life to telling people what he believed to be the truth, had a certain humility about it when he wrote things like, 'We know only in part,' and 'We are as looking through a dark glass.'[4] There is a story I like that illustrates this.

> A man was called to be a witness in a court case. When his turn came, he was sworn in by the bailiff with the usual words: 'Do you swear to tell the truth, the whole truth, and nothing but the truth, so help you God?' He answered, 'Listen, if I knew the truth, the whole truth, and nothing but the truth, I would be God!'

The limitations to my knowledge notwithstanding, I do believe in the mathematical principle of the excluded middle, which, stated mathematically, says, 'If (A) is true, then Not (A) must be false.' In other words, a statement and its contradiction cannot be true simultaneously. Of course, in ordinary daily life, determining the truth of a statement may be no easy matter, but ideally, the principle still holds.

Stating that one knows the absolute truth not only reeks of arrogance, it denies a need for learning. I had a friend from Texas who told me that, back home, they had a saying: 'Lord, help me to always seek the truth, but deliver me from those who have found it.'

The nature of autism

The emotional deficit – the bedrock trait

When I first discovered the fact that I was autistic, I had to think of a way of describing myself concerning human emotions. I had to face up to the fact that, as most humans experience and show them, I did not have any. Not wishing to mince words, but to get to what I saw as the central issue, I described myself as 'an emotional idiot',[5] a designation that I was not surprised to see used by other newly self-discovered autistic people. This was modified, in a response to a communication with Temple Grandin, when she referred to having an 'emotional deficit'.[6]

I came to regard this as being the bedrock trait defining autism[7] and discovered that I was not alone in that, being seconded by respected professionals in the field. Dr Lorna Wing[8] wrote to me, in referring to autistic people, that 'They have to learn through the intellect because of disability affecting intuitive emotions.' Dr Paul Shattock,[9] wrote that we are '...those with an intellectual rather than an emotional response to problems, the 'head' as opposed to 'heart' people...' From this, it is not unexpected that all of the perceptions we have and the decisions we make are totally intellect-based. As the old saying goes, 'When all you have is a hammer, the whole world looks like a nail.'

While I use rationality to reach the conclusions to which I come, I am often amazed at how, in others, these conclusions elicit an emotional response. This would indicate that, while emotions are not rational in themselves, they can respond to things that are and that even though rationality is by its nature non-emotional, emotions need not be non-rational.

There are other disorders that are often associated with autism. These include attention deficit disorder, sensory integration disorder, lack of ability to communicate, being fidgety, learning difficulties, lack of social skills, and also mental retardation. I should like to refer to these later.

The autistic spectrum

This title implies that autism is not a single, monolithic syndrome, but includes a wide variety of manifestations. The word 'spectrum' connotes a range of traits other than the common trait of the emotional deficit. By what measure, for the individual person, is the place on that spectrum determined? I have heard that the degree of mental retardation is often used, but I believe this to be misleading. All too often, retardation is measured using tests requiring some ability to communicate. Lack of this ability is something separate from being retarded, which is a deficiency of the intellectual functions. There are many autistic people whose communication is quite limited, but who nevertheless show themselves to be quite intelligent. Put another way, just because a person says nothing, it does not mean that he or she has nothing to say.

Ability to communicate

In light of this, perhaps a better criterion would be ability to communicate. This would place, at the high end of the spectrum, those with Asperger Syndrome (AS) who, by definition, have full capability to communicate with others, both oral and written. Next would be those with high-functioning autism (HFA), who can communicate, but only in a limited way. An example of this would be someone whose eloquence in speech is limited, but who writes expressively. At the low end would be the *savants*, who, as a rule, cannot communicate at all in words, but who exhibit an almost superhuman ability in one small area, which requires a rote ability that would beggar that of most people.

Note that I place AS people at one end of the spectrum. There are those who would consider them a separate category, but I think that the differences between AS and other autistic people are of degree rather than kind, although it might appear to be the latter.

Asperger Syndrome and autism

Much has been made of a list of 'differences' between those with AS and other autistic people. One, in particular, involves the willingness to engage in social contact. Non-AS autistic people tend to shrink from that, or even avoid it altogether. Does this mean that the AS should not be considered autistic? I bring this up because I have, in mathematical terms, categorized HFA as a subset of autism and AS as a subset of HFA, while this type of distinction would imply that they are disjoint sets.

I have to go back to the definition of AS. The distinguishing trait is having the full range of communication – spoken as well as written. How does that impact the sociability problem that I mentioned above? Most human conversation that I have observed does involve a bit of disagreement over something. Most of the time, this is very calm and quiet, and over a trivial subject but it is still, nevertheless, disagreement. Examples: what to have for dinner, what color drapes to get, which TV shows to watch, and so forth.

If one party to such a conversation has difficulty finding the words to express his or her thoughts, then there is not a level playing field. One feels at a disadvantage in even making one's wishes or ideas known, let alone asserting them. The result can be perceived as social withdrawal. Yet this is not done for emotional reasons, but actually as a very reasonable survival tactic.

On the other hand, the AS, with their relative ease of speech communication, do not feel at that much of a disadvantage. The give-and-take of conversation is not taken to be a threatening situation. This makes 'sociability' much easier. Yet there is a subtlety at work here. Before my discovery of being autistic, I would at times wind up with my foot in my mouth and I could not understand why.

This did lead to a certain reticence in any interactions with others. After that discovery, I came to realize that there were definite identifiable limitations on my ability to interact, and these were the result of the limitations on my ability to understand people and their motivations. I had, after that, a greater ease in person-to-person speech. I still sometimes put my foot in my mouth, but could usually figure out why. (This can vary from a social gaffe to boring people without being aware of it.) To my understanding, this is the explanation for the greater sociability of AS people. It is twofold: an ability to communicate and also a confidence in that ability.

This is not an exercise in semantics. It bears heavily on dealing with public policy, especially with respect to such things as insurance coverage and government benefits programs for the disabled. In many cases, autism is covered while Asperger Syndrome is not. If the diagnosis is the latter, then benefits could be denied. That would be due to the fact that a condition is not specifically on their list. (This is sometimes unavoidable due to the fact that eligibility determinations are made by administrative rather than professional people.) In many such instances applicants, in order to get coverage, will put down something that is on the list. In the case of AS, a person filling out the form could very well put down 'autism' with a clear conscience.

The pitfalls of using 'traits' to profile

All too often, character traits are used to profile someone who has some disorder or other. As an example, consider the following list of descriptive qualities:

1.   He grew up in a dysfunctional family.

2.   He was a 'loner', even as a child.

3.   He has never had a really close friend, in the sense of a confidante.

4.   He puts a high premium on logic and rationality.

5. He does not show emotion.

6. He did not seek out close relationships with women.

7. The few relationships he did have with women turned sour.

8. As an adolescent, he did not share the interests of other adolescents.

9. He was never interested in 'guy' things, such as sports or cars.

10. He excelled in mathematics and the physical sciences.

11. He feels comfortable in the company of outcasts.

This is a fairly accurate profile of me. It is also the profile of Theodore Kaczynski, the infamous Unabomber who, to vent his irrational rage at the technology that he believed was despoiling the environment, sent packaged bombs to a number of people he believed had a prominent hand in that process, causing injuries and even deaths. To the best of my recollection, I have never done anything quite like that!

Yet this is the approach that is usually taken in diagnosing mental conditions. It can be seen in the Diagnostic and Statistical Manual (DSM) of the American Psychiatric Association (APA).[10] I have several difficulties concerning their approach. For one thing, they list a number of traits and say that anyone who meets a certain subset can be considered as having this disorder. Apart from this being a method that could be called 'choose-one-from-column-A-and-one-from- column-B', I have a more precise complaint. Suppose that it gives a list of 12 traits and then says that any seven of them could qualify. This means that two people could be said to fit the diagnosis if they share only five traits. I realize that the 'S' in DSM stands for 'statistical', but the example I give yields the sort of probability I would not wish to bet on.

Advanced courses in mathematics start with a review of set theory, because this is fundamental to the categorization required in mathematics. In this discipline, all elements of a set are required to have at least one common trait. For example, to be included with the even integers, a number has to be exactly divisible by two. I tend to be uneasy with a scheme that would allow, under certain circumstances, 37 to be included or 86 to be excluded.

Another problem with this approach is that, given a set of traits, the identity of the disorder is not uniquely determined. In my autobiography, I demonstrate how the same traits can be exhibited by both the schizoid and autistic personalities.[11] There is a further disadvantage in that the set of traits could very possibly describe something that is not a disorder, or at least nothing requiring therapy.

When John Hinckley, who shot President Ronald Reagan, was declared insane at his trial, he was consigned to St. Elizabeth's Hospital in Washington DC, a maximum-security mental institution. I read in the newspaper that, when a hearing was held to determine if he could be allowed unsupervised daytime releases, it was opposed on the grounds that he suffered from, among other things, the Narcissistic Disorder.[12] I looked this up in the DSM, and found the following traits:

1. He has a grandiose sense of self-importance.

2. He is preoccupied with fantasies of unlimited success, power, brilliance, beauty, or ideal love.

3. He believes that he is 'special' and unique and can only be understood by, or should associate with, other high-status people.

4. He requires excessive admiration.

5. He has a sense of entitlement, i.e. unreasonable expectations of especially favorable treatment or automatic compliance with his expectations.

6. He is interpersonally exploitive, i.e. takes advantage of others to achieve his own ends.

7. He lacks empathy; he is unwilling to recognize or identify with the feelings and needs of others.

8.   He is often envious of others or believes that others are
      envious of him.

9.   He shows arrogant, haughty behaviors or attitudes.

With all due respect, in official Washington there are so many people
fitting this profile that Mr. Hinckley would have had no problem
blending into the background.

 Besides all this, I was amazed to discover that the DSM contained
something called the 'Mathematics Disorder', which is characterized
by the following: 'Mathematical ability, as measured by individually
administered standardized tests, is substantially below that expected
given the person's chronological age, measured intelligence, and
age-appropriate education.'[13] When I was in elementary school, since
pocket calculators were as yet unthought of, 'Mathematics' consisted
of being drilled in arithmetic computations, and words fail me to
describe how much I hated it, although I could do them, but not
without errors. My MA degree in mathematics notwithstanding, I still
can do them now, but again not without errors, and always carry a scientific pocket calculator with me. Did I have the Mathematics
Disorder?

 I once saw a 'test' by which, if one could see certain traits in
oneself, there was a possible psychiatric disorder that could be associated with that trait. One of these traits was that the person's mind is
constantly in operation. I know that this is a trait for which I must
plead guilty. Yet in my mind doing this, I have made many discoveries
and gained many insights, all of which have enriched my quality of
life. What kind of 'disorder' is that?

 Perhaps the approach I have taken to this topic is a bit too
light-hearted, considering the stakes that are involved. On the basis of
diagnoses that are made using these criteria, therapies could easily be
ordered that are inappropriate or even unnecessary.

Explanations of some autistic traits

Because NT people look at the mannerisms of the autistic with their own world-view and according to their own values, they often tend to misinterpret what they see. Jasmine Lee O'Neill, in various places in her book,[14] discusses some of these in considerable detail, but I should like to briefly address them with an eye to correcting these misapprehensions.

Lack of eye contact

Many autistic people have exceptional peripheral vision. My wife has it and my ophthalmologist tells me that my field of vision is great for a person of any age. Sometimes, when talking to a person, something else requires my attention. While looking at that, I am still able to clearly see the person to whom I am speaking. I am not avoiding eye contact with him or her, but am taking advantage of the fact that I can see both quite well.

Apart from the obvious benefit of being much more aware of one's physical environment, there is another that bears directly upon a favorite hobby of mine. Ever since the fall of 1964, whenever the opportunity presented itself, I have sung with very high-powered choral groups, many times together with symphony orchestras. I have a memory problem in which, although I remember the big picture and all of the major details, small details tend to fall through the cracks. For the kind of music we have done, this deficiency is critical. There are the questions of how long a note (or a rest) is held, whether there is a dotted rhythm or not, and so on. If I am to sing together with the rest of my section, I need to pay close attention to the printed music in the score. For this reason, despite my love of opera, I have never sung in opera choruses. Since I would have to be part of the stage action, carrying and reading a score would be somewhat incongruous. The music would have to be memorized in precise detail. Yet even in chorus concerts, because the conductor might want to vary the rhythm, with things such as retards and accelerations, I have to pay attention to what he or she does. My very good peripheral vision allows me to look at the score and also follow the conductor's motions in the upper part of my field of vision.

Perceptiveness

This could be defined as the faculty which enables one to discern similarities and differences that many others tend to miss entirely, or at least overlook. This proved indispensable in my study of advanced mathematics, and has greatly aided my penchant for reasonable categorization. Looking back, it is a faculty that I have had as long as I can remember. It is possessed by many autistic people.

This ability played a significant role in Einstein's development of The Special Theory of Relativity, believed by many to have been autistic, mostly because of his failure to form mutually satisfactory personal relations. I shall attempt to explain this without going into too many of the details of the physics that are involved.

It has been known, since the time of Sir Isaac Newton in the 17th century, that when one measures the position and velocity of a moving object, one gets different readings if two measuring devices are themselves moving with respect to one another. The set of formulations, which relate those two measurements, is what is meant by Relativity. In 1877, two physicists named Michelson and Morley made measurements of the speed of the light coming from the sun, with one measuring device moving toward the sun, and the other away from it. To the astonishment of all physicists, including the experimenters, the two values of the speed of light were identical. The problem remained unsolved until 1905, when it was explained by the new formulations developed by Einstein for his Special Theory of Relativity.

What is germane to this topic are the circumstances under which Einstein made this discovery, which changed forever the way we perceive the structure of the physical universe. Unable, after receiving his doctorate, to obtain a professorship at a university in either Switzerland where he lived, or in his native Germany, Einstein was forced to take a job well below his abilities. He was an examiner in the Swiss government patent office, essentially looking for flaws in people's inventions. Since it did not take him all day to do the work that they gave him it was, practically speaking, in his spare time that he pondered the implications of things such as the Michelson-Morley experiment. Consider this: he had no library, no laboratory, and no colleagues with whom to discuss things. He had no esoteric knowledge; whatever he knew was known to all other physicists. As with the old saying, he saw what all others had seen, but thought what none of them had thought. He had perceptiveness.

Sensory overload

This can be best described as the feeling one gets when another person scratches his or her fingernails on a blackboard. Many autistic people have special problems of this nature. This is to be expected, since brain damage or improper brain development could possibly also be accompanied by nerve problems. The child, or even the adult for that matter, should not be taken to task for reacting this way, even if it is something of a public embarrassment. Some of the autistic react that way to certain colors, some to certain sounds, others to certain types of touches, and so on. Some autistic people, while they cringe from the touches of humans, like close contact with animals.

For both my wife and myself, tickling is sheer torture. She dislikes vocal music because she reacts that way to the frequencies in the soprano range. In my case, I find myself very uncomfortable with back rubs and baths (I much prefer quick showers), especially the whirlpool kind. I know that they are supposed to relax but instead, they make me nervous.

Ironically, I am not bothered in the least by fingernails scratching on a blackboard.

Mind blindness

This is another trait possessed, in varying degrees, by autistic people. It is the inability to discern the true intentions of others. This is not to be confused with inability to 'read minds'. That would be the power to precisely know the words, pictures and thought processes in the mind of another. There exists no credible scientific evidence that there is such a faculty.

This is another matter altogether. There are nuances in facial expressions, body movements, tones of voice and so on, through which people express their thoughts and feelings non-verbally. It is as though these nuances form a code. In order for these thoughts and feelings to be understood by others, there must be a method of 'decoding' which means recognizing patterns in these non-verbal communication methods.

NT people, largely, are all capable to a great degree of recognizing such patterns. (For this reason, it usually takes a very skilled charlatan to be able to fool many people through being able to disguise his or her true intentions.) Imagine, on the other hand, not being able to visually or aurally decode such patterns, thus missing completely the 'signals' sent by others. This is where the 'blindness' part comes in; the patterns cannot be 'seen'. Autistic people have this difficulty to some degree. There are those who, from experience, have developed a 'file' of these nuances, so they are able, to some extent, to 'read' people.

Many have not. I am one of them. This is ironic since, in my many cerebral interests, I deal with nuances and have to be able to think metaphorically and analogously. Yet when it comes to personal interactions, I take things totally in a literal manner. I have no way of knowing when someone is serious or is merely 'kidding' or 'teasing'. I take people at their word. Given this, the possibilities to flimflam me are unlimited. So, if anyone pulls the wool over my eyes, it's nothing to brag about.

Yet once I realize that I have been deceived, the deceiver rarely gets a second opportunity to do that. The initial deception can be easy because of my inability to see, in people's mannerisms, warning signs that I have not noticed before. However, once I come to the realization that I have not been dealt with honorably by an individual, the characteristic of perceptiveness comes into play and, as far as that person is concerned, very little gets by me.

One of the more serious consequences of mind blindness is that I am defenseless against what I call 'ceremonial politeness'. Perhaps 'defenseless' is too strong a word, because it implies that I am under attack. While I am certain that there is no such intention on the part of an NT person, it does accurately describe the state in which I see myself when that sort of situation arises.

For example, someone makes an offer to do something and another cheerfully thanks him or her. There is no intention on the part of the first person to do it, nor does the second person expect it to be done. Also, someone says, 'Drop by anytime you're in the neighborhood.' The other says, 'Of course I will.' The second person would not dream of just 'dropping by', and the first would be offended if he or she did. None of this is said in so many words, but there are 'signals' passed between the two that make this completely understood.

What if one person is NT and the other autistic? The latter has neither the antenna, the receiver, nor the decoder for such 'signals'. No pictures need be drawn to depict the uneasy social situation that is a result. Since the vast majority are NT and this is a faculty they take for granted to the extent that they use it without thinking about it, I cannot expect them to give me much slack, if any. All I am able to do is explain to people whose friendship I want to keep that, with me, they need to be explicit and specific. I also keep a growing set of 'warning signs' that hopefully would help me to recognize the kind of situations that the NT recognizes instinctively.

From my observations, ceremonial politeness is a veneer that can be used to hide a vicious streak in someone. A perfect example in literature is the finale of Alexander Ostrovsky's Russian play *The Storm*, from which the Czech composer Leŏs Janáček took his opera *Katya Kabanová*. The matriarch of the family is a domineering virago. At the end of the opera, she has been responsible for the estrangement of her young ward, the emotional disintegration of her son, and the suicide of Katya, her daughter-in-law. She turns to the villagers, who had helped search for Katya and found her body, bows and says to them, 'Thank you, thank you, good people for your services.'

The parents of young autistic children need to inform their relatives and friends of the absolute necessity of being explicit and specific with that child. This is something that, for those parents, there must be the constant awareness of practicing it themselves.

'Stimming'

This is a jargon term used to signify repetitive behavior. All too often, this is confused with obsessive-compulsive disorder (OCD). For that syndrome, a person does things repeatedly because of an irrational fear that they are not being done correctly. An autistic person, on the other hand, will do this if he or she finds an activity from which pleasure is derived. That activity is repeated for the purpose of achieving repeated pleasure. There is one such habit of mine that may very well annoy others. When I think of something very wise or clever, I cannot resist the desire to tell it to everyone I know.

Sometimes this term is also used to denote talking to oneself by oneself. (Generally speaking, if one does this, then one only has oneself to blame should the conversation get boring.) For the autistic, the harmlessness, or even the benefits of this can be illustrated by something I heard from a schoolteacher. She told me of an autistic boy who she had in her class. During recess, the boy would not join in any of the group games, and would sit on the side by himself, talking quietly to himself. Sometimes, when the teacher came near him, she could hear him, by himself, going over the material they had just covered in the classroom.

Before she had learned what autism was all about, her NT mindset and her professional training told her that this boy was painfully lonely, that he lacked the self-esteem required to be sociable, and that he needed to be made to be part of the group. She then told me that, after having learned about the nature of autism, she realized that the best course of action would be to just let him be. To this, I added that she also needed to ensure that the other children did not physically bully him because he was a loner.

I should like, at this time, to repeat this book's thesis: autistic people have a way of creating their own happiness, even if it is not in ways that the NT would consider as being happy.

Possible causes of autism

Brain Damage

One area where I have had to modify my opinion is that I attributed my own autism to brain damage caused by infectious diseases (the likely culprit was pertussis) and I had believed that this was the only type of cause. Some parents of autistic children, with whom I have spoken about this, have told me similar stories. Their children had experienced various ailments, all of which resulted in a very high fever for at least a week. When the fever finally subsided, they found themselves with a child whose personality had changed radically, as mine had done.

The part that got damaged was the center for the intuitive emotions, which is in the temporal lobe. I happen to be acquainted with a young woman named Shari Lynn who has written a fascinating story related to this.[15]

At the age of 17, she was driving a car borrowed from a friend. Ordinarily, she always fastened her seat belt but the belt buckles on this car would not lock. Her car was struck by someone who had run a red stop light and not being properly belted, she was thrown from her car and suffered extensive injuries, including concussion damage to the left temporal lobe of her brain. For a period of time her life hung in the balance. After a while, following much therapy, she recovered, but with one exception: she had not only lost the ability to deal with emotions, but had no recollection at all of how she ever did. To summarize, the accident, causing that kind of brain damage, had rendered her autistic.

When the brain is damaged, it is not a precision operation. Whether from infection or from physical trauma, it is very likely that there may be a number of centers that are injured. For each of these, the corresponding faculty will be impaired. If the brain center for the intuitive emotions is not damaged, then whatever the deficit for any other faculty, the person will not be autistic. There are people who suffer from mental retardation, who have learning difficulties or who lack social skills, but who are not autistic.

A genetic cause

For a long while, I believed brain damage to be the only cause of autism. I did not believe that there was a genetic component. One bit of evidence for this was that, in my case, I am the only one of all of my blood relatives who is autistic. To those who had children that were born with autism, I pointed out that infectious illnesses can affect a fetus *in utero*. (I would have to say that, if autism were genetic, one would not be born autistic, but would be conceived autistic.) To those who pointed out that there exist clusters of autism in families, my explanation was that there could be a genetic susceptibility to the infections that cause autism.

Recently, I was told about the identification of a gene that has something to do with brain development. Should that gene have a condition that would cause improper development of the center for emotions in the temporal lobe then, in that case, autism could definitely be inherited. Thus, I came to realize that it is not an either/or situation, but can be both.

Autism has been referred to as a developmental disability. This would be true quite literally if it was due to a defect in the brain development gene. That would be impairment of direct development. If, on the other hand, it results from damage due to infectious disease or physical trauma, this could be considered a reversal of development.

I see here an interesting ethical question. Since this is not an either/or condition, the two points of view are not mutually contradictory. Why should there be such a heated controversy?

The vaccine controversy

There is one topic, on the possible causes of autism, around which there is no small amount of dispute. This involves the use of vaccines. One sore point in particular is that of government requirements for vaccinations as a prerequisite for school attendance. While the problems are quite real, this has, unfortunately, led to a host of true believers on both sides. Some, including parents of autistic children, blame vaccines for their children's condition. The vaccines most blamed are usually 'cocktails' of multiple vaccines, such as those for diphtheria, pertussis, and tetanus (DPT) or for measles, mumps, and rubella (MMR). In the extreme, they see a conspiracy between government and the vaccine makers. Others denounce those who oppose these immunization programs, or even question them, as a threat to public health, saying they put school populations at risk by placing non-immunized children in their midst. While I do not pretend any expertise in epidemiology or immunology, I should like to offer my two cents' worth on this issue.

As I understand it, vaccines are supposed to give the recipient a weakened form of the disease. Through some biological mechanism, the body then builds up defenses that protect it if there were to be an invasion by the full-blown version. The statistics show that this approach has resulted in the eradication, or at least the control, of many infectious diseases that had plagued humanity. Smallpox and polio are excellent examples.

Unfortunately, there are some who have such a great susceptibility to a disease that even the weakened form in the vaccine is sufficient to trigger the disease itself. It might appear that, for one who is vulnerable, if he or she is not vaccinated, then he or she would be a prime candidate for contracting the disease. To minimize this, perhaps tests should be devised to detect such susceptibility. Another precaution could be to give the vaccinations singly, over a period of time, instead of in a cocktail, which could be quite an assault on the immune system. My view on the controversy is that, while statistically vaccines are definitely beneficial, for the parent of a child with such a vulnerability who gets sick after a vaccination, this is very cold comfort indeed.

Emotions

Theirs and Ours

'Love means suffering!!!'

The words in this very dogmatic pronouncement are those of Kurt Mazur, who was, until recently, music director of the New York Philharmonic Orchestra. He said that, with precisely that much emphasis, during an intermission interview on a televised concert of the NYPO. I normally pay little or no attention to the pedantic blather on these features, usually reading or daydreaming while waiting for the music to resume. This one, though, caught my attention as if by a jolt. 'He's out of his tree,' I said to myself, 'Love should be something that alleviates suffering.'

However, I then realized that this was a sentiment that I had heard all too often from NT people. It is a notion that I, and those like me, categorically reject. Perhaps that is why, so often, NT people consider us 'incapable of love'. Ironically, when I give them my comment about alleviating suffering, they agree, yet while accepting that intellectually, they nevertheless embroil themselves in liaisons that cause suffering!

There is one type of situation in which love and suffering could be related. This is when the object of that love is in danger and the lover must put him or herself in danger of serious injury or even death for the sake of the beloved. An example is a mother defending her child. That coupling of love and willingness to suffer seems quite logical; at least it is not illogical.

Before comparing and contrasting how both groups, the NT and the autistic, view this topic I first feel I should clarify my qualifications to discuss human emotions. This is a very reasonable point to address, since I have already admitted to not having any of my own.

I shall use an analogy of a physicist who wants to know the locations in an atom of the electrons orbiting the nucleus. The physicist cannot experience that directly, in the sense of seeing those positions and measuring distances. What he or she must do is look at the frequencies in the radiation spectrum of a particular atom. While the details are greatly beyond the scope of this book, I am able to point out that he or she can look at those frequencies, and use a well-known functional relation (at any rate, well-known to physicists) to detect those electron positions. During my lifetime, I have observed the effects of human emotions on people's happiness or unhappiness (alas, mostly the latter). This puts me in a knowledgeable position.

The physiology of love

This title seems to imply a dry, clinical approach to an emotional topic, but it does enable one to understand what is going on by sorting things out. In my autobiography,[16] I wrote about three types of love, and identified them by their Greek words. These were φἶλος (*philos*), which comes from the intellect, αγάπη (agape), which comes from the emotions, and έρος (*eros*), which I had identified as coming from the sex hormones but which, more specifically, comes from our primal instincts.

Each of these has its own center in the human brain. *Philos* is located in the cerebral cortex, which contains the circuitry for the highest functions, such as intelligence, rationality, and the making of ethical choices. Except for the more advanced primates, such as chimpanzees, who have a rudimentary form of it, this is unique to humans and is what separates us from the other animals in a qualitative manner. *Agape* is located in one of the temporal lobes (which one depends on whether one is right-handed or left-handed), and is a faculty possessed by all higher animals. *Eros* is located in the limbic area of the brain (from the Latin *limbus*, meaning 'border'), which is the most primitive part of the brain, and is the section that we share with all of our vertebrate predecessors on the evolutionary ladder.[17] This has profound implications concerning non-autistic human behavior.

I had long believed that the expressions 'loving' and 'being in love' represented a distinction without a difference, and there was only one use that I noticed for such a distinction. When a man wants to copulate with a woman who is reticent about that prospect, he manipulates her by saying 'I love you' often enough to make her believe that he considers her to be something and someone special. After she allows him to do his will a number of times, he gets bored and moves on to other things. She then confronts him, reminding him of how he said he loved her. He manages to avoid any unpleasantness by telling her, 'I do love you, but I'm not in love with you.' While she tries to sort this out, he finds an escape route. (I am sure that there are many examples of this kind of manipulation with the genders reversed – another step forward for gender equality.)

However, the physiology does give us some genuine differences between 'loving' and 'being in love'. *Philos*, which comes from the intellectual center of the brain, and *agape*, which comes from the center for intuitive emotions, have some things in common. As forms of 'love', they are persistent and so durable. They can also be a continuing source of satisfaction over the long haul. *Philos*, however, has a rational basis and tends to come about after it becomes apparent that there is minimal possibility of it leading to suffering. Conversely, *agape* is not guided by rationality. Pascal[18] noted that 'the heart has its reasons of which the reason knows nothing'. (As an Asperger individual, I have tended to interpret this as a complaint.) Since reason is not present to recognize possible warning signs, the opportunities for future suffering are significant.

Eros is synonymous with being 'in love', and is also characterized by something quite vague called 'chemistry'. As I mentioned earlier, this resides in the limbic area of the brain, the home of the primitive instincts. These are purely situational in origin, which means that they are reactive to specific external stimuli and, most important of all, they are ephemeral. I would hope that no decisions of long-term consequence might be made on the basis of this, but this is exactly what people seem to do. They will not even consider a partner unless there is 'love at first sight'. George Bernard Shaw ridiculed this by saying, 'When two people are under the influence of the most violent, most insane, most delusive, and most transient of passions, they are required to swear that they will remain in that excited, abnormal, and exhausting condition continuously until death do them part.'[19] It is noteworthy that Shaw used the word 'passion,' which comes from the Latin word for suffering, for this kind of situation would seem to guarantee this.

Three dangers can be seen here. One is that the choice of a life-mate can be made on the basis that Shaw so eloquently describes, which can cause one to be terribly wrong about that choice. Another is that a man or woman, because the 'magic' is not there, might dismiss a potential partner with whom there could have been a love-basis (either *philos* or *agape*) for a lasting union. The last is that, when the deluding bond of 'chemistry' wears off, the couple is left wondering, often with increasing bitterness, 'where the magic disappeared to'.

There is an analogy that, I believe, highlights the difference between 'love' (from either the heart or the head) and 'in love'. Consider a quantity of phosphorus. It catches fire with extraordinary ease and, when it does, burns with such brilliance that it cannot fail to dazzle. However, before long the flare-up is gone with no sign that it had ever been there, except for a smudge where it had burned. This is 'in love', or the 'chemistry'. 'Love' is like a small amount of coal. It ignites only with patience and diligence. Nobody even notices the time when it does start to burn, but it burns for a long time, giving warmth, if not much light, let alone brilliance. The time when its glow can best be seen is when it is totally dark.

On the topic of mating rituals

A man and a woman meet. They, at first, find each other easy to be with, or at least not uneasy. They also find each other easy to talk to. This is not to say that they have all their interests in common, but at least neither finds any of the other's interests abhorrent. What interests they do share they mutually cause to grow in their enjoyment of them. Where their interests diverge, each discovers from the other something new to enhance their own existence. While they may have different beliefs, they find that they share common values. Any limitations each might have are understood and accepted by the other. Together they find ways to work around them. Each finds the other appealing in an aesthetic sense, but as time goes on, there is a physical dimension added to this. They are open and above-board with each other. There are no unrealistic expectations or plans to change the other person, realizing that what you see is what you get. They also treat each other with kindness, generosity, and respect. Their sporadic meetings become more frequent, and before too long, after they have gotten to know each other thoroughly, they realize that they want to share each other's company continuously.

What I have just described could be characterized as spontaneous mutual attraction. If this is to be called 'love', then where is the requisite suffering? Is this the way NT people come to love each other? It seems not! Indeed, from my observations the process is quite the contrary.

Sincerity and dependability

In *Yeoman of the Guard*, Gilbert and Sullivan put in a trio, in which it is said, that, unless there are sneaky tactics used, a man has no chance at all to attract a woman in whom he is interested. Quite likely the same would hold for the genders reversed.

In that same mindset, during my youth there was a popular song, in which each verse ended with: 'You have to know the tricks of the trade.' There are also many books and magazine articles on the rules to follow, as well as techniques and tactics to 'get' someone from the opposite sex interested in you.

This attitude pervades all NT entertainment about 'love', and it all comes down to one single word – manipulation. By any definition of that word, it says that you have to get someone to do something which, if left to their own devices, they knowingly would be unlikely or unwilling to do. This says a great deal about the self-image of people. The implication is that someone who is in full possession of his or her faculties, who has his or her feet on the ground, and who is able to sort things out in a clearheaded manner, could not possibly have any interest in you. Thus, to get him or her interested in you, you have to manipulate that person. But it is logical that anyone with any self-respect, and not given to kidding him or herself, would get no satisfaction from a liaison built on such a thing as manipulation. Why would anyone want to face what happens when the object of that manipulation comes to his or her senses?

This manipulation is not only needed to arouse the original interest, but also to maintain it, lest the other person lose interest. (One could go further and state that, without such continuous manipulation, this loss of interest is inevitable.) This appears to be true even after marriage. Couples, even with children, are constantly beset by worry about 'losing his (or her) love,' or 'having the fire go out'. The bookshelves and magazine racks bristle with advice on how to keep this from happening. The proliferation of this often conflicting advice is evidence that it seems to be ineffective.

From this, it can only be assumed that 'love', as described, is insincere (because it is so much dependant on manipulation) and undependable (because it can vanish without any warning). How can anyone possibly have any confidence in the sincerity or dependability of some other person, since it is something that is so ephemeral and contingent upon manipulation? There has to be some awareness, even subliminal, that there has been such manipulation. Along with this, is a fear that some danger might lie ahead. This fear, far from being neurotic, is quite rational. Why should anyone be willing to make any kind of commitment under such conditions?

For something that is sincere and dependable, we must look to hate. When someone hates you, there is no doubt as to his or her intentions, nor is there any hidden meaning behind his or her words. Also, as to dependability, one never hears, 'I have fallen out of hate with that person.' In the popular song from Rogers and Hammerstein's *South Pacific*, we are told that one has to be taught to hate.[20] This is unrealistic thinking. Because of its sincerity and dependability, hate comes very easily to people, while love is very difficult both to initiate and to maintain.

The insecurity of people, resulting from the necessity of manipulation's fragility of duration, appears also to require that one's choice of a mate must be endorsed and ratified by one's friends. It is as if any confidence in that choice is incomplete without an *imprimatur* of the form, 'Wow, where did you get him (or her)?'

Challenges

I have often heard it said, by both men and women, that 'Marriage is the graveyard of love.' To put it less elegantly, there is the question, 'What can someone eat that suppresses the sex urge?' to which the answer is, 'A wedding cake.' I had often wondered why, given this manner of cynicism, men and women want to get married. Some try to solve this by entering into 'alternative lifestyles'. From my observations of these arrangements, while they do start with all of the advantages of marriage and none of the disadvantages, it is not too long before they have the reverse: all of the disadvantages and none of the advantages. So again the question, 'Why do these formal and semi-formal unions so often destroy what they are supposed to consummate and enhance?' The answer came to me during a conversation.

I was, not too long ago, standing around with a group of friends and acquaintances, discussing things about the human condition. When the topic came around to problems with human mating, one of the women said, 'Men and women both look upon each other as challenges.' All those around, except me, nodded in assent. I can understand that this might be a good thing if we talk about the problems of people and what can be done to help them. In this case, the man or woman could rise to the challenge to help the significant other find a solution to the problem. However as the conversation continued, it became clear to me that this was not what they meant; they referred to a person him or herself being the challenge. Even if no problem exists, the nature of the other person's very being can be thought of as a challenge. This, it seems to me, leads to the creation of some problems where none had existed before.

Suppose a man comes to know a woman who would love him gratuitously. She is no challenge and offers him no opportunity to prove himself so he is likely to dismiss her as a possible partner. This could be an unfortunate choice, as she might very well have been a very good one for him. She also affords him no opportunity to brag to his friends about his 'conquest' and how he 'overcame her resistance'. In other words, how he was able to manipulate her.

What of the woman who is considered a challenge because she does not give any signs of interest in him? I suspect that it flatters her to be thought of as a prize to be won. In doing that, she encourages his manipulation. What happens if this comes to fruition and the two get married? The challenge has been met, the prize has been won, and the trophy is on the shelf. After a while, won't it be time to move on to the next challenge? I have heard many a woman lament that, not too long after the wedding, her new husband loses interest in her, and she wonders why. She should wonder no longer!

Likewise, consider a man who, even with the kind of foibles that all people possess, is fine just the way he is. To a woman, he is no challenge so she is likely to dismiss him as a possible partner. Again this could be an unfortunate choice for her. To prove herself, she creates a challenge by planning to make a number of changes in him whether such changes are needed or not. Of course, if she were to announce this beforehand, or show signs of trying to make those changes, she likely would alienate him before they got married. She therefore postpones that project until after the wedding, pretending that she loves him exactly the way he is. This is also a form of manipulation. After the wedding it is time for her to start to work on her project of 'improving' him or to re-create him in the image she would like of him. Now he is unable, without considerable legal difficulty, to walk away from his inevitable disillusionment. I have heard many a man lament how, not too long after the wedding, his new bride would sharply criticize him for the exact same personal qualities for which, before the wedding, she had praised him, and wonders why. Given this, he should wonder no more!

The extreme cases of this are those in which the object of desire is a true challenge. For men, it is the woman who has a deserved reputation, figuratively speaking, for hanging men's scalps on her bedroom wall. For women, it is men who, for one reason or another, could be called 'worthless'. These men could be alcoholics and/or drug addicts, compulsive gamblers, men with a history of abusing their mates, men involved in organized crime, or men who seem to be able to get sexual satisfaction only from prostitutes. The spur to such choices appears to be: 'I am going to succeed where other men (or women) have failed.' This has got to be the ultimate challenge.

Given what I have written earlier about manipulation, I cannot grasp why men and women alike believe that they have to manipulate to get what they could have just for the asking. Perhaps, in that instance, there is no challenge. Is there any way to avoid all these pitfalls and to have marriage be something that reinforces love rather than kills it? The only thing that I can see is to bide one's time until there is someone with whom there is a spontaneous mutual attraction. But then, what do I know?

A parable of the cog wheels

There is a certain type of machine, deemed essential to the survival of our civilization that is totally dependent for its operation on two critical cog wheels. If their gear teeth fail to mesh, or grind when they do mesh, then the machine will operate either poorly or perhaps not at all.

In the best of all possible worlds, or if the only consideration were the smooth operation of these machines, then all cog wheels would be made to be interchangeably alike, so that the gears would mesh perfectly, no matter which two cog wheels were used on a particular machine. This is not the best of all possible worlds, nor is smooth machine operation the only consideration.

As a result, the manufacturer, who has a worldwide monopoly on the production of these cog wheels, makes each one with its own unique set of gear teeth. This, of course, introduces no small amount of complexity into the matching of the cog wheels for installation on a particular machine.

The obvious bad case is that for which the gears on two cog wheels are so badly mismatched that they would grind with any attempt at meshing. Installing these two on the same machine will have to result in that machine not being able to operate at all.

When is love unconditional?

From the usage that I hear of the expression 'unconditional love', it would appear that it involves total acceptance of another person regardless if that person is, among other things, an abuser, an addict, or a career criminal. (Note that this is not gender-specific.) In every case with which I am familiar, the result is the suffering of which maestro Mazur seemed to speak as being an essential part of love. The word 'unconditional' implies a certain degree of selflessness, but the interpretation that was given does not speak well of love as something to be sought and, in any case, the resulting suffering can only be characterized as self-inflicted. There is a word for this: masochism.

Being a cat lover, I had often wondered what sort of character traits would be required of someone in order to properly relate to a cat. One absolute essential is the ability to give love without worrying about whether or not one gets it back.

I have found that most NT people cannot even understand this attitude, let alone accept it. They consider love to be incomplete unless it is requited. However, this says that love is diminished if unrequited. Does this not put a condition on it? Then, by definition, it is no longer unconditional. Furthermore, when the condition of reciprocity is not met, there arises that totally illogical phenomenon of 'love turning into hate'.

Perhaps one problem is that people equate being unconcerned with lack of reciprocity with being indifferent to it. There is a difference of no small consequence, and I should like to use my cat as an example. Any number of times she would be walking across the room. I would call to her, but she would not as much as turn her head to acknowledge me. I felt no pangs of rejection. Yet sometimes, when I would be lying on my couch, she would jump up and curl up against me, or when I would be doing something like working with my computer I would feel her tapping on me with her paw. I would see her sitting there, purring, and I would stroke her coat (it's so luxurious that I ought to charge people to do that). I knew that she did these things, not because she had to or needed to, but because she wanted to. Since I had no expectation of this, it was like receiving an unexpected gift. I would imagine that there could be similar rewards for two people who, in this sense, are able to love unconditionally.

There is another aspect to this notion of a love that is unconditional, or should be. Given that a desire for reciprocity is a condition that is placed on one's love, there is an interesting viewpoint, from a rather unimpeachable source, on why this would be a cause of suffering. The point that it makes is even stronger than those I have made. In the ethical teachings of Prince Gautama Siddhartha, otherwise known as the Buddha (Sanskrit for 'the enlightened one'), there is a word, *thanha*, which means craving, grasping, or desire. According to this moral theology, a 'love' that is given in the expectation, or at least the hope, of being requited, is attempting to satisfy one's own desires, so there has to be some selfishness involved, which is thwarted if there is no reciprocation. This leads to actions that cause suffering for oneself and for others. The Buddha taught that happiness must be found, not in others, but in oneself. This way, any expression of affection, trust, or commitment that one has for another will cause no suffering.

A while ago, I saw on one of the Internet lists devoted to autism, a post from a mother of two children, one NT and the other autistic. She had asked each of them, 'Why are you special?' The NT child's response was, 'Because I am loved.' The response of the autistic kid was, 'Because I love.' Is this not the unconditional love of which I wrote?

The 19th century French poet, Alphonse de Lamartine wrote: 'To love for the sake of being loved is human; To love for the sake of loving is angelic.' Does this kind of love come so easily only to the autistic? I am not saying that it does, but I am not denying it either.

A short clarifying comment

What I have heretofore written on this topic has been called by many, and not without good cause, the 'battle of the sexes', or the 'war of the sexes'. One might note that I have used paired terms such as man/woman, he/she, and so on. This might be construed as meaning that the behavior and values that I have described are limited to heterosexual couples. I would like to correct that misconception. I have, at one time or another, had occasion to observe gay and lesbian couples and, from my observations, the only thing that they have done with the war of the sexes is to turn it into a civil war.

The Story of Ed and Alix

How we met

Alix and I met on the Internet.

That conjures up an image of someone logging onto either a chat room or an on-line introduction service with the words, 'Hello. I'm...and I'm lonely. Is anyone out there lonely too?' There invariably follows at least one response. The instigator then chooses what appears to be a few likely prospects from the group of respondents. It doesn't seem to matter that one may have encountered a serial killer or rapist (maybe both), a swindling fortune-hunter, or a 'black widow' gold digger. These are all out there, and have been known to frequent such sites in their hunting expeditions. There follows an exchange of personal information (to say the least, unreliable) about age, education, ancestry, income, social status, assets (of course, there are no debts or other liabilities), interests and hobbies, and eventually a photograph, very likely retouched and 15 to 20 years out of date. (One might wonder why, if all these are as good as they are purported to be, this person has not attracted a mate locally and has to resort to this sort of thing.) While *caveat emptor* (let the buyer beware) is generally ignored in this quest for a possible end to one's loneliness, it should be the

guiding principle, in this of all situations, because no truth-in-adver-
tizing laws apply to personal interactions. I often wish that I could,
somehow, be able to sell tickets to their first face-to-face encounter.
(There is a classic *New Yorker* cartoon which shows two dogs, one
sitting on a chair in front of a computer and the other on the floor. The
first dog says to the second, 'On the Internet, nobody knows you're a
dog.')

I brought all of that up as an egregious example of how it did *not*
happen. The actual story, while more prosaic, is not without some
interest.

We each had, individually, signed on to a few Internet list services
that were concerned with autism. For a while, both Alix and I posted
to these lists on a more-or-less regular basis. Impressed with what she
had to say, I would sometimes send a response, as she sometimes did to
mine. Both of our responses, at the time, were to the lists. Then, on one
occasion, there was a thread (a series of posts and responses with a
common subject) whose subject escapes me right now. For reasons that
I cannot now remember, I decided to reply with the following story:

> Some man dies and goes to his judgment. St Peter takes one
> glance at his record, slams the book shut, and sends him
> straight to hell. The Devil takes a look at his record, and says,
> 'Boy, you're rotten even for the kind of people we get here.
> I'm consigning you to the lowest part of the pit. I don't trust
> you, so to make sure that you get there, I'm assigning one of
> my devils to escort you down there.' On the way down, they
> pass a wedding ceremony. The bride is stunningly beautiful.
> 'Who's that?' asks the new arrival. His devil replies, 'He's a
> world-famous mathematician, who has solved problems that
> have eluded the best mathematical minds for upwards of three
> centuries.' The man says, 'There's no justice, even in hell. I
> have to burn forever at the bottom of the pit, while he gets to
> spend eternity with that gorgeous woman.' 'Silence!' shouts
> his devil, 'How dare you question her punishment?'

Alix sent a response to the list, 'I could marry a mathematician.' I
replied to her, this time privately, 'You could?' She replied to me, also

privately, 'Yes, if he were the right kind of mathematician.' That was the beginning of a private e-mail correspondence between us. After a while, she gave me her home phone number and I would call her once a week or so. It was like a long-distance date.

During this time, we got to know each other. We began mostly to swap ideas on many topics. She disagreed with me from time to time, but gave specifics so those disagreements gave me a great deal of food for thought. Our ideas seemed to come pretty much from the same place. (After all, as Vulcans, we were both from the same planet!) Before too long, we also started to swap our personal histories, and from that it appeared that our outlooks on life meshed quite well. She had always said that, in rural Maryland where she lived, the job opportunities were limited, and she also disliked the cold climate. I had often suggested that she relocate to south Florida, where I live, but it never got beyond that. Over time, I got to like her quite a bit and did develop the beginnings of serious intentions about her. From the phone calls and e-mail messages, she seemed to do likewise. Could this not be called a spontaneous mutual attraction?

Personal difficulties I had to overcome

Before continuing with this story, I have to digress. As one might know, both from reading my book and from any private conversations, I attribute the failure of my first marriage to our joint ignorance of my autism.[21] Also, in one of the last chapters, I stated that the inability to make one woman happy over the long haul was my life's one great failure.[22] In addition, when I speculated on the likelihood of a future close relationship with a woman, the probabilities varied from the minuscule to the imperceptible.

There was even a chapter in which I waxed rather cynical about the entire idea.[23] My experiences with NT women, since writing that, had not caused my cynicism to wane. Every possibility had turned sour, usually over a divergence in fundamental values. (In retrospect; lucky me). I had come to think that perhaps a cloistered monastery would be too crowded. This was not a notion that I pulled out of the proverbial hat, but was just about set in concrete by an experience that I had even while that divorce was in progress.

Before I made my conversion to Catholicism, I had to convince myself that I agreed with the Church's teachings, including the one on the indissolubility of marriage. The key Biblical phrase was Matthew 5: 32. There are many translations of this, but when I saw this passage in the original Greek, I became convinced that the only rationale for dissolving a marriage was if it were invalid in the first place.

Thus, when I undertook my first marriage, for me, that was it. It was 'One strike and you're out.' As such, I did not even contemplate the possibility of a second. For ten years, I had no doubt that I had hit the ball over the wall. Then, as the difficulties stemming from our mutual ignorance mounted, I turned around and there was the ball in the catcher's mitt. I had come to greatly regret ever having stepped up to the plate.

During the last months of the marriage, I saw in my church bulletin, that at some other church, there was a support group for Catholics who were separated or divorced. Hoping to pick up some pointers for dealing with a situation I had never envisioned, I went to a meeting. There were a few women, myself, and one other man. At the outset, we were asked to say a few things about ourselves. The other man said that this was his second sojourn with a group like this. I suddenly realized that my worst nightmare would be a second marriage that would be a replay of my first. (I use the word 'nightmare' as a figure of speech. In the sense of a dream so frightening that I would wake up in a panic, I have never had a nightmare.) I must point out that, at the time, I had not come to fully comprehend the ramifications of being autistic.

The supposed fact that an indissoluble union of mine had failed, was actually a source of comfort for me. After one mass, following my divorce, I said to my priest friend, Father Neil, that I was glad that I would never be able to do something that stupid again. He then shattered my complacency by telling me that, having gotten to know both of us, he saw quite a number of impediments that would enable me to get an annulment from the Church should I wish to marry again. I did not know whether to be happy or frightened. In my analysis, the marriage had failed because: 1. I was extremely difficult to live with, 2. I had blindly entered that marriage because I was a poor judge of character, or 3. both of these. I could not see how any of this would be improved in a second attempt.

This perception, using the metaphor of the cloistered monastery, was reinforced when I had occasion to learn about 'mixed marriages', meaning a union of an autistic person with one who was non-autistic. In every case that I encountered, if the wife was autistic (and the autism was known to both), it could and did turn out OK; if the husband was the one on the spectrum, then there were serious problems that were very difficult to deal with. Since I happen to have the inconvenient Y chromosome, this was no small factor in believing that the only close female companionship I would ever want would be my cat.

It is interesting to note that Temple Grandin, in her book,[24] advised an autistic person, if he or she wished to marry, to do so with either another autistic person, or someone with some other disability. Readers of my autobiography will recall that I dismissed this idea out of hand. I still cavil at some 'other' disability. If I were to marry, say, a blind woman, then I would have no problem understanding her limitations and adapting to them. However, would she understand mine? I strongly doubt it. As one autistic list subscriber once wryly posted, '…it is not a normal disability'.

Before going on, I have to emphasize that I would not 'look' for a liaison of any kind. 'Looking' is done to fulfill a need. By my nature, any interaction I have with others is because I want to, not because I need to; just like a cat.

The story continues

After a year or so, in April 1998, I got into a disagreement with Alix over something on an irrelevant topic that was important only in the sense that it made me strongly question my assumption that we shared common values. Since that assumption had been so fundamental to my opinion of her, it raised that specter of a replay of my first marriage.

The disagreement got so intense (mostly over values) that, after a while, she told me that she did not want to talk or correspond with me anymore. After a short while, my bafflement subsided and I gave thanks that my worst nightmare had been eluded. In any case I never expected to hear from her again. There followed a number of attempts at interactions with women that varied only in their degree of ultimate disappointment, which I got over in short order.

Toward the beginning of April 1999, I was startled to see her e-mail address in my on-line inbox (a list of incoming e-mail messages). I was consumed with curiosity more than anything else, so I opened that one first. It was mostly small talk chit-chat, asking what had happened to me in the last year, and so forth. I replied very much in the same vein, telling her about the publication of my autobiography and other things, mostly trivia. I was glad to hear from her and believed that we could perhaps be civil friends, if nothing more than that.

I did have to wonder why, since we had parted on such a discordant note, she wanted to resume our on-line correspondence. After three or four weeks, my curiosity got the better of me and I asked her why she wanted to revive our friendship. She mentioned a few items, which I have forgotten but, at the last, she wrote that she missed me. I asked the next obvious question: if that were so, why had she broken off with me in the first place? I was totally unprepared for her answer.

She replied that, given my commitment to Catholicism, and the 'one-strike-and-you're-out' rule (those were her words), she felt that any future for us was hopeless. I had to remember that, in our earlier correspondence, she had asked me many questions that would have gauged that commitment. As one who converted for purely ideological reasons, that had to be quite deep. Also, this 'hopelessness' would indicate, that at the time she decided to end our correspondence, she had been quite seriously considering the possibility of marriage. Being of a logical bent, or at least not illogical, she saw no sense in prolonging anything and decided to break it off. By that time, I must have communicated my value system to her, fully and accurately, because she certainly knew which buttons to push.

This actually made me quite happy because I realized that it was all the result of an unfortunate misunderstanding on her part. She had made assumptions that were simply not true. I then explained to her what impediments and annulments were all about, and how Father Neil had assured me that I would have no problem getting one. Since the topic is not a simple one, there had to be a number of e-mails back and forth over a couple of days but, after it was explained to her satisfaction, things returned to the way they were a year earlier. That's all it took. We did not discuss marriage at that time. It took a reversal of her fortunes to force that to happen.

A time of decision

I have mentioned before that job opportunities for Alix were quite limited where she lived. For one thing, she did not have any financial resources at all, so she had to take what she could get and had neither the time nor the money to qualify herself for anything she might really want to do. As a result, for ten years before this, she had worked as a live-in governess for the children of very wealthy parents.

She had often said, in her posts to the lists, that she never wanted to have children of her own because of having been mistreated as a child by her parents. (One of her favorite sayings was: 'The most difficult thing we have to do in life is to survive our parents.') For one thing, she feared that any children of hers would turn out to be just like her parents. For another, being very controlling types, she feared that they would bypass her and micromanage the raising of their grandchildren.

Yet she was more than a mother to these children entrusted to her, whose parents obviously looked upon them mostly as hindrances to their social lives. All too often, she had to make decisions that should have been made by the parents but who could not be bothered to do so. This highlights to me a truth about parenting: it only takes minutes to become a parent, but decades to be one. Alix, who had never become a mother, certainly had been one to her young charges.

One redeeming feature of these jobs was that she did get a place to live that was rent-free, but in May 1999 she received notice that her job was being terminated and that she also had to vacate her apartment. It was then that I repeated my suggestion of her relocating. I offered to take care of all the details, including picking up the tab. It was an offer that I hoped she could not refuse, and ultimately she did not.

This had to lead to getting into the nuts and bolts of what would be the relationship between us. Before proposing marriage to her, I told her that I loved her in the only way that it was possible for me, but with all of the intensity that I could bring to that. I had no idea what her response would be. For all I knew she would write that what I said was insufficient, or that she looked upon me as no more than a father figure or an older brother.

It was quite a pleasant surprise to see her write back that she reciprocated totally, but it was something else that she wrote that I found gratifying. In reply to my 'the only way that it was possible for me', she wrote that she understood me completely because, 'When we talk about love and happiness, our meanings are totally different from when those others use those words.' Since I, in making that overture, had expected nothing in return, it was like getting a totally unexpected gift. I then asked her to marry me and she accepted. I could not resist asking her, 'Does this mean that I am the right kind of mathematician?' She replied, 'Yes, Ed. You are the right kind of mathematician.'

I flew up to where she lived toward the end of May. We got all of her belongings packed and I rented a truck. After the Memorial Day holiday weekend I drove the truck and she drove her car, together with her cat. While we did rough it, it was made less difficult by my having bought a couple of hand-held FM radio transceivers that we used to communicate en route.

The trip took four days, but all three of us managed to survive. (My youngest son graciously had agreed to keep my cat during my absence, two cats of his own notwithstanding.) We were quickly ensconced in my condo apartment and I discovered all kinds of creative ways of utilizing my available space in a manner more efficient than I had needed to before. The two cats got to be good friends with each other as only cats do. When they are not individually ignoring the existence of the rest of the universe, they groom each other, wrestle with each other, and chase each other. As an example of how talented and creative Alix is, before I went to get her, she had designed and built web pages for each of our cats.

There was only one barrier remaining to getting married. My divorce had left me with a large number of debts and Alix wanted assurance that, should I die, as my wife she would not be liable for them. Realizing that this was far from being unreasonable on her part, I consulted the attorney who handled my divorce. He told me that in Florida, a person, even when half of a married couple, is liable only for those debts for which he or she personally signs. That being taken care of, we were married in a civil ceremony on 26 June 1999. For an announcement, Alix designed and built a web site which she posted on the Internet.

About marriage

This is a good place to explain my views on this topic. I should like to respond to those who favor 'alternative lifestyles' and those who wonder why a person, who considers himself a committed Catholic, would not only marry in a civil ceremony but also without first obtaining an annulment from the Church.

As to alternative lifestyles (which are often a euphemism for cohabiting without marriage), I have one observation. Anyone who would come into such an intimate aspect of my life without a formal commitment could also walk out without a backward glance. While the sympathy of others would be welcome, I have no logical claim on it, so I have no cause for complaint if I do not get it. Conversely, any woman who would allow me into her life without such a commitment is, in effect, telling me that she cares not if I were to exit on a moment's notice.

There will be the claim that such a commitment can be made without a legal document. While this is true, I have to look back on an experience I had while in the Army. After I became an officer I would often have to sign out a piece of equipment to be used in a training exercise. I would usually turn it over to a sergeant to actually use in the training, but regulations required that the formal responsibility had to be taken by a commissioned officer. When I turned it over to that sergeant, I would take a page from my notebook and write out a hand receipt to be signed by the sergeant. It would be returned to him when the item was returned to me. In short order, I discovered that many sergeants would say things like, 'Sir, if my word isn't good enough, my signature isn't worth a damn.' At first, I would just order him to sign it. I later thought of a very good conversation-ender: 'Sergeant, should this item be lost, damaged or destroyed while in your care, and I have to justify being relieved of responsibility, your word is not evidence; your signature is.' I never got an argument after that.

There is also the question that, for a married couple, there are both government and corporate benefits that are not available to two cohabiting single people. I do not consider this to be unjust. Both the government and a corporation have resources that, while impressive, are not unlimited. Expecting taxpayers or shareholders to subsidize someone's succession of live-in sex partners is not fair. As my wife, Alix would have those benefits. Isn't that the logical thing for me to want? I had, at the time, no idea how important that would turn out to be.

As for the civil ceremony, some time before I married Alix, I asked Father Neil about this issue from a purely hypothetical point of view. I told him that, if I were to marry, I would want my wife to be eligible for benefits immediately. If I had to wait for the year to 18 months that it takes to process an annulment then that would put her at no small amount of risk. He told me that, as long as I state my intention to seek an annulment, I could marry in a civil ceremony and still receive the sacraments. This requirement has been satisfied. (The nature and ramifications of annulments, I have discovered, is little understood by most Catholics, even educated ones.)

This is a good point at which to discuss both the purpose of marriage and the family and the need for some kind of public recording. The Church teaches that its function is for two people to form an indissoluble union for the purpose of providing each partner with someone who can give friendship and support, and to provide for the proper nurturing of any children that might result. Engels,[25] on the other hand, said that this purpose was for the holding and transfer of property. Question: which one of them is correct? Answer: they both are.

In the first case, it can be asserted that the union is made when the couple involved resolves to do what it takes to achieve those purposes and make promises to each other to that effect. Could this not be said to happen when they become engaged? If that be so (and the couple are serious about wanting God's approval), would a public ceremony and recording be required? Not necessarily. This is even reflected in the Church's view of two things. First: the Church does not marry anybody; the two people marry each other. Second: two people who live in a remote area where there is no priest can, by making such vows to each other, contract a valid marriage. (There are those who might cavil at this because the vows, not made in a ceremony, are not made also to God, but I doubt that God would have had His hearing aid turned off.)

What of Engels' assertion? The state does have, for the maintenance of civil tranquility, what lawyers call 'a compelling interest' in the orderly holding and transfer of property. The family is the instrument that has been selected for this. To be able to settle any property disputes peaceably, there would have to be a public recording and the marriage ceremony serves that purpose. This could be called 'rendering unto Caesar the things that are Caesar's'.[26]

Complementary compatibilities

Resolution of disputes

Since no two people are exactly alike, even to the choices that they make, when two people live in close quarters there will be disputes from time to time. Alix and I are no exception to this. From my observations, the NT way of resolving this takes two forms. One is for the two to state their respective pieces in unyielding ways, until one or the other gives in. Failing that, they stew about it for a good while. The other is for one partner to establish dominance at the outset and to unilaterally make all decisions after that. Alix and I, being Vulcans, are very much an exception to that.

I have mentioned earlier that we managed to clear up the misunderstanding over annulments via e-mail. This was, of course, necessitated by the great physical distance between us at the time, and due to the complexity of the issue, took a couple of days to resolve. Now we occupy the same residence, but we found out that this was a good way of handling such matters. We each have our own computer with our individual e-mail account. Although there is now only a one room distance between us, we discuss the matter by e-mail. Unlike the NT way, with their spoken confrontations, we each can take the time to get a good long look at the words of the other without appearing 'weak'. Our responses to each other can be measured, and can include such questions as, 'What do you mean by that?' or, 'Do you think that this is what I meant?' In every dispute we have had, it has only taken three or four e-mail messages back and forth, over a half-day or less, to come to a resolution that is satisfactory to both of us.

There is a notion, very much in vogue today, that men and women have difficulty communicating with each other because they, in effect, speak totally different languages. The words may be the same, but the meanings are disparate, if not contradictory. A metaphor that is used is that they come from different planets, the metaphorical thesis of a popular book.[27] Alix and I, both being Vulcans, do not have that problem. She had remarked that when we use words like 'love' and 'happiness,' our meanings are different from those of the NT. Of course, when NT men and women use those words, their meanings are also different from one another; our meanings are the same. A final point on this communication topic is that, unlike the NT, when something bothers each of us about the other, we address the actual cause instead of masking it behind some red herring. If the topic is too touchy, we use e-mail. In my case, it gives me an opportunity to either explain myself if it cannot be fixed, or to clean up my act if it can.

This idea about the communication problem between men and women is not new. Twenty-five centuries ago, Plato realized that. In contrast to the snake-oil solutions offered by modern commentators, in his *Republic*, he offered the only logical solution: that they live in separate communities and get together only for sex.

Dealing with danger

There is a chapter in my autobiography[28] in which I discuss my high pain threshold and lack of any appreciation of danger to myself. As an example, many times I will inadvertently cause myself a slight injury, such as banging my leg against a table. If the skin should be broken, that could be serious. Because of my diabetes, however under control it is, the danger of infection is not insignificant. Since I take little or no notice of any associated pain, I often do not realize what has happened and discover it only after infection has set in. One reason for this is that the cut is usually in a spot not readily visible to me. Before Alix moved here, the only one who could have seen it and then warned me about it, had a vocabulary limited to 'meow'.

Alix, during our long-distance phone calls, had told me that she had similar problems. I would offer the possibility that we could each watch out for the other. Since our marriage, this is precisely what has happened. I know of a story that illustrates this.

> In both heaven and hell there is an eternal, unexhausted smorgasbord, set with all the delicacies one could possibly ever desire. However, each person's elbows are ossified so that he or she cannot bend them. It is not permitted to eat from the table directly with one's mouth. What then is the difference between heaven and hell? Those in heaven are the people who have learned to feed each other.

A new career

I have written about Alix' work as a governess. That was not the only type of job that she had held. When she had just turned 18 years of age, she enlisted in the US Navy, was trained, and worked as a dental technician. (For this reason, while very anti-war, she has great respect and empathy for our veterans.) On two occasions, in California and

Maryland, she worked as a wild animal handler. In the latter job, she trained a bear. I should like to tell about her latest occupation.

When Alix and I were writing to each other at the outset and I had suggested relocation to south Florida, she had asked me what the employment opportunities were like. In particular, she inquired about openings for security guards. This surprised me because I would never have guessed that she would be interested in that. After we were married, she told me the story of how she came upon that notion.

At the age of 27, her father was working as a security guard. From time to time, he would forget his lunch and Alix would ride her bicycle to take it to him. She saw the kind of work he was doing and decided that she would like to do that also. (It is worth noting that, while growing up, she had many bad experiences with her parents but she did not transfer this dislike to things associated with them, as many NT people do.)

After we had been married seven months or so, she began once again to express interest in pursuing that line of work. It was not as it was, a dire necessity. On my income alone, we were able to live comfortably, if not opulently. In Florida, a license (called a 'D license') is required, and there is a 24-hour course of instruction that is a prerequisite for a state-approved exam. Alix was certain that we would not be able to afford it. I convinced her to find out just how much it would cost before we gave up on it. In April 2000, she did. At that time, I had just received a royalty check for my autobiography. It was slightly more than enough.

Alix then searched the Internet for schools that offered the course, found one relatively close to us, and signed up. When she came home from taking the exam, she said, 'I flunked.' I was somewhat taken aback by that. Then she showed me her exam paper: 98 out of a possible 100. I guess that I failed to notice the grin that accompanied her announcement of failure.

We went to the nearest state licensing office with her credentials and a certified check for the fee. On the way home, she told me that, in two years, her license would have to be renewed, and that a 16-hour course was needed for that. I asked her how much it would cost to take that course. When she told me, I realized that there was just enough left over from the royalty check to cover it. I urged her to take that course so that, when renewal time came about, she would already have the necessary certification. She took that course at the same school, but did not do quite as well: 93 out of a possible 100.

I told Alix to take her time looking for a job, and she did. After all this time spent to qualify, neither of us wanted her to have to take any old job that offered itself. After making a number of inquiries, she applied for and was accepted by a major global security company. It was not, as she said, something that she had pined and yearned for, but it also became the source of no small amount of personal satisfaction. This was evident each time she left for work. She was a sight to behold, but then I guess that I was always something of a sucker for someone who looked good in a uniform.

An admitted error

In several places in my autobiography,[29] I state that the only basis I could possibly have for a close friendship would be one that is based on common interests. This would certainly have to be the case with someone I would want to marry. After all, what would we talk about? This assumption was to be put to the test and proven wrong.

When Alix and I were e-mail penpals, before we got married, we shared many ideas and viewpoints (in the sense of how one looks at things and evaluates them). When I brought her to Florida and we were married, I noticed that there were many differences between us, some of which, given what I just wrote, could prove unsettling.

My bent is intellectual; hers is aesthetic. I express myself, on a day-to-day basis, mostly through speech (and some writing); she expresses herself through her computer, by e-mail and the web sites she designs and builds. We have different tastes in music. Mine goes to Wagner operas and Mahler symphonies; hers to country and rock of the 60s and 70s. We have different palates; I prefer dishes with a number of different flavors, she prefers a blander fare. (My diet is somewhat restricted as a Type II diabetic, while hers is not. Also, her metabolism is in a much better condition than mine.) We also have different tastes in reading; I prefer things with and about ideas, she likes paperback novels. I alluded above to my favorite entertainment; hers are movies about stock-car racing, and when she could go, the races themselves. (If she could, she'd drive in those races.) Our backgrounds are also quite dissimilar; she, though raised in a midwestern city is, by temperament, a rural WASP (for the unfamiliar: white, Anglo-Saxon Protestant). I am an urban Catholic with immigrant parents. When it comes to plants, she has a green thumb; I have a brown thumb. I am an analytic thinker; she is a visual thinker. I take the long view of things; she is a 'here and now' person.

Yet aware of these dissimilarities, in the time that we have been together, I always sensed that there was a basic underlying similarity that was evidenced in our correspondence before we married. (Perhaps it was our common autism, although we had different forms of that.)

I would often comment on that to her but wondered if she agreed with me, because she did not comment back much. Then on one occasion, all of the uncertainties were resolved when, completely unsolicited, she sent something to me that she had come across while surfing the web. It was a picture of a Siamese kitten sitting next to a miniature schnauzer puppy. The text over the picture read: 'We may be different.' Underneath it said, 'But we're two of a kind.' I would not attempt to even guess the number of words that were conveyed by that one picture.

What does this mean with respect to the assumption that I had made about common interests? It is that a much more important compatibility is that of values. It has since occurred to me that shared interests would, in my case, require that we should have common intellectual capabilities. In retrospect, there was only one woman that I could have married who was my intellectual equal: my first wife, in that marriage that ended in such dismal failure. (In light of this, it was a fortunate thing for Sherlock Holmes that Irene Adler married someone else.) In our household, I am the intellectual and Alex is the artist. Is this not a good example of complementary compatibility?

One recent incident humorously pointed out our shared values. The very small car that I had bought, used and driven for four and a half years, had seen better days and was likely to soon have seen all of its days. My problem was that I was in no financial position to buy a replacement. One Saturday, we went to the lot of a local dealership 'just to look'. We saw a car, a mid-sized, four-door sedan, which totally met our needs but where the price was still out of my reach. I did not haggle but they eventually gave me a deal I could not turn down, which included an unrealistically high trade-in on my old car. During all of this, Alix stood by and said nothing, except to give short pieces of advice at what turned out to be strategic points in the negotiations. After I had signed all the papers, Alix confided to me that, when she had lived in rural Tennessee, 15 years before, she had traded horses. Alluding to an advertizing slogan for a very upscale car, as we drove from the dealer's lot, she grinned and said, 'Well, Ed, whose house shall we drive it by first?'

Health

When it comes to doling out punishment, the toughest hanging judge in the world is a bleeding-heart softie compared to Mother Nature. This is an observation that I failed to make until it was almost too late.

My first crisis

Sometimes the worst thing that your body can do to you is to tolerate your bad habits. Mine did that with a metabolism that many would envy, but which turned out to be illusory. From my father, a North German, I had inherited a tall, lean body. My maternal grandmother, a Russian immigrant of the 'lower' classes, held to the notion, common to people of that kind of ethnicity, that this was a bad thing and tried, without success, to fatten me up. The end result was that, for most of my life, no matter what or how much I ate, I was still quite thin.

During my adolescence, this stood me in bad stead with girls of my age. Part of their notion of a 'dreamboat' was a boy who was very muscular. (These days, he would be called a 'hunk'.) The logical assumption on my part was that the girls considered me unattractive so I did not date in high school. This caused me no loss of sleep.

Later in life many envied me for my ability to 'pig out and stay thin' but they need not have bothered because Mother Nature took their revenge for them.

At the age of 57, or thereabouts, my metabolism took a dramatic shift, and I put on a great deal of weight. There were consequences of this. In about three years, I developed Type II diabetes, acid reflux, and hypertension. My primary physician prescribed medications that, for a while, kept these under control and therefore I believed that there was no cause for alarm and that the bad effects were purely cosmetic. (I was unconcerned about this because my marriage had long since turned bad and I was not interested in attracting anyone.) In the fall of 1994, I began to revise such notions.

At that time, I started to notice that my sense of balance was starting to get worse. It had been bad since March of 1956 when, during an Army training exercise, I suffered concussion damage to both inner ears from a grenade explosion. I have also had in each ear, high-frequency hearing loss and a constant ringing. Presuming that the balance problem was a worsening of these conditions, I was examined in April 1995 at the Miami Veterans' Medical Center and was told by the specialist, after a number of tests, that my ear problem showed no signs of being exacerbated and so it was suggested that I consult with a neurologist. On doing so, he ordered both a magnetic resonance imaging (MRI) of my brain and brain stem and two Doppler ultrasound readings to test the blood flow through the carotid arteries (in my neck), and the blood flow around the inside of my head. The verdict was that the carotid flow was normal, but that in the vertebral and basilar arteries that feed the back and base of the brain, the blood flow had all but ceased. In addition, the MRI showed that there had been some brain atrophy in the area affecting balance. There were two more disorders discovered: close-up double vision and diabetic neuropathy in my legs below the knee. This is basically a loss of feeling.

The blood-flow problems in my brain were the result of a combination of diabetes and hypertension, both of which were traceable to being overweight. I might add that, with the onset of the poor balance, my blood pressure and glucose readings had gone up, causing my primary physician to increase the dosages of the medications I had been taking for those problems. Also, my cholesterol readings had exceeded the danger point of 200. If something were not done, I was either going to die, or worse, wind up in a condition in which I would wish that I were dead. My weight problem had escalated from the unsightly to the deadly. Unquestionably, something had to be done about those excess pounds.

My daughter, when she was pregnant with her fourth child, developed gestational diabetes. Having a very responsible position in her company, her management insisted on diet counseling. (This worked very well for her and for my new grandson.) She came to realize that she had been doing a lot of things that were flatly wrong, and correctly assumed that I had been doing likewise. Acting on her advice, I had my primary physician refer me to a group of registered dieticians and nurse educators. (I might point out here that the reputable ones will not counsel you without such a referral. They want access to all of your medical data before deciding what to do with you.) The program consisted of seven hours of lecture and counseling, after which I was given a diet-and-exercise regimen that was tailor-made for me. I determined to follow it with no deviation.

There were a number of surprises in that regimen. For one thing, I discovered the extent to which exercise is overrated in weight control. I looked at the calories that are burned off by an hour of weight-lifting or a couple of miles of jogging. They are all gotten back from one jelly doughnut. (An excellent example of denial: eating doughnuts and then putting artificial sweetener in your coffee.) Besides, a history of asthma precludes such activities. On two occasions where it was required, doctors have refused to sign permission forms to allow me to use exercise equipment, so I have taken to daily walking and/or swimming. The diet part consisted of three modest meals and three controlled between-meals snacks. These were to prevent the appetite from being ravenous at mealtime. This ravenousness is no small problem for those who rely on strenuous exercise. I have seen many men and women fight a losing battle against a weight problem because of what I call 'work-out followed by pig-out'. I purchased a kitchen scale and some measuring cups, and for about four weeks weighed and measured everything I ate. After that, I developed a 'feel' for what needed to be done.

I started this regimen at the end of June 1995. By January 1996, I had lost 55 pounds, a few pounds below my median ideal weight. That was a bit much, so since then I have put back about five pounds, putting me close to my ideal weight. I have maintained that since. The physical rewards were obvious. As I lost the weight, my blood pressure, blood sugar, and also my cholesterol dropped accordingly, eventually to normal levels. The dosages of the medications I was taking for diabetes, reflux, and hypertension were reduced until they were eliminated altogether. I have been getting normal readings in all my physical examinations. In fact, my primary physician tells me he does not see numbers as good as mine on most men half my age. While I still have some close-up double vision, my sense of balance has improved greatly. The most amazing thing is that over the past couple of years, I have come back from diabetic neuropathy, which I understand rarely happens.

There are also psychological benefits that are impossible to quantify. Not only is there a feeling of personal well-being, but even the world around one looks better. Sometimes, when I go shopping in a supermarket, I pick up a five-pound bag of potatoes, and contemplate that I used to carry ten or eleven of those on my person. I should mention that it was not so much what I did, but the way that I went about finding out what to do.

Many 'fad' diets promise weight loss. Apart from the fact that they are not geared as mine was to the individual person, they usually contain within themselves, the seeds of their own failure. When a label says, 'One size fits all,' it usually means that it doesn't fit anybody. There is an initial weight loss, but that is usually due to loss of water. The weight comes back, invariably as fat. There are also pills to take that have the same effect, but often have deleterious side-effects. All of these are geared to hoping to lose weight while retaining a lifestyle that is still basically unhealthy. It goes to a mindset of wanting to have one's sins and heaven as well.

Besides my regimen being my very own, it involved a dramatic change in lifestyle, from one that was unhealthy to a healthy one. (Once I had accepted that nothing short of a lifestyle adjustment would suffice, the rest was not difficult.) This embodied taking control of my life. There is, these days, a great deal of psychobabble about self-esteem. I am hard pressed to think of a greater self-esteem enhancer than taking control of one's life.

Alix's crisis

I mentioned, when I first wrote about our marriage, that one motivation among many others, was that I had wanted Alix to avail herself of my company's spouse benefits. It was a good thing that I did. Before I go into the episode behind that remark, I should like to summarize some other things that were done. It must be remembered that there was well over 20 years of catch-up to do.

The first thing to happen was that, using our benefits, I got Alix some new eye glasses. Her old prescription was all wrong. Amongst other things, asthma, allergies, and periodontal problems were discovered. All of these have been, or are being treated.

I then had Alix get a complete physical exam by my primary physician, an internist, her first in more than 20 years. This was on 13 July 1999. Though he normally does not do this, he took a pap smear because he did not like what he had seen during what is euphemistically called a 'pelvic exam'. (I was always under the impression that the pelvis was a bone, so it should be under the purview of an orthopedist rather than a gynecologist.) When the results came back, he called them 'very bad', and used no small amount of his influence to make an appointment for her to see a gynecologist the very next day for a biopsy.

The biopsy, which was done in the gynecologist's office, came back, as he and the internist had both said, 'very bad'. It was called *in situ* cancer, which means that it was not yet invasive. He wanted to do a 'cone biopsy'. On August 9, I took Alix to the hospital to get some pre-op tests (blood work, an EKG, and a chest x-ray). The next day, I took her at 5.30am, to have the surgery done. The doctor saw me afterward and said that she did very well, and that he would wait for the pathology report before deciding where to go from there. He further said that a decision as to full-blown surgery would depend on the pathology report and would also have to take her age into consideration.

I spoke to Alix in the recovery room (for this procedure, she had been given a general anaesthetic), and she said that she would like to go ahead and have everything taken out, including her ovaries. She said that even if it were not yet invasive, it likely would become so and at that time, she would not be any younger. Also, if bad things showed up now in one place in her reproductive system, it would only be a matter of time before they showed up elsewhere. Her clear thinking, even in such a stressful situation, has never ceased to amaze me.

One problem that Alix did have is that, while her anti-clotting levels were normal, she had a bleeding problem that was at the time unexplained. As such, she had been pretty weak. The only problem I had was keeping her from doing things that, given the situation, I should have been doing. However, Alix has had no family for very many years and, being autistic, had not developed the kinds of friendships where she could routinely call on someone for help. She had become used to doing everything for herself, no matter how dire the circumstances. That is a very tough habit to break.

Anyhow, Alix got stronger, although she did sleep a lot (due mostly to her internal bleeding). We were waiting for the pathology report, but major surgery was all but absolutely certain. I am glad we were able to catch it when we did. As the internist had inferred, it should have been taken care of years before, but none of Alix's jobs had any benefits, and she was always too poor to afford medical insurance on her own. Resulting from this, she had never seen a doctor for anything that was not immediately life-threatening.

Alix had told me that, when the internist saw what had so frightened him, he took her to considerable task for 'letting' it get to that point. I called him and told him that she was unlike his usual patients, who had either money or coverage, and who thus should have had it treated in a timely manner. 'Allowing' it to get to the stage at which he saw it was not the result of either denial or procrastination, but of poverty. I had always been something of an advocate of national health insurance but, as a result of this, I have become a true believer.

On 18 August, Alix went to see her gynecologist to get the results of the biopsy. In a way, it could be said that there was good news and bad news. As for the good news, he told her that the cone biopsies were negative for being invasive. The bad news was that they were as close to that as it gets.

I had mentioned that she felt that anything less than having everything out right now would only be postponing problems, so she and the doctor agreed that this is what would be done. (With her usual, perhaps unusual sense of humor, she told people, 'I'm gonna get spayed.') She was aware of the fact that this would cause immediate menopause, but she was convinced that she would have no problem dealing with that. I agreed with her and, from what I had gotten to know about her, also shared her optimism. During a conversation we had, she agreed with me when I summarized what she had said – since she would be trying to keep up with possible future malignant eruptions, anything less would be like shooting at a moving target. Alix's surgery was scheduled for Tuesday 31 August, first thing in the morning. That plan would have to be changed.

To reiterate what I said earlier, it is good that we got married when we did, so that Alix became eligible for those medical benefits. If this had been put off too much longer, we would be looking at something much more serious.

Because she had a problem with internal bleeding, it was essential that she not be subject to any sudden motions while she healed from the earlier cone biopsy surgery. In spite of meticulously sticking to that, including modifying her sleeping arrangements to preclude such motion, she had, after steadily improving, a severe bleeding episode on Sunday night, 22 August. The following Monday morning, we reported this to her gynecologist who called her in to see her that afternoon. The bleeding had stopped by then. However, there had been two cancellations for surgeries scheduled for Tuesday, so Alix's surgery was moved up a week to 24 August.

I should like at this point to give an example of Alix's sense of humor, which she had kept up throughout. To our marriage, we brought her cat, a neutered male, and my cat, a spayed female. Monday afternoon, Alix came out of the bedroom, wearing a big grin, and told me that she had just been talking to my cat. The cat, she said, had told her that she had been there and done that, and had come through OK, so not to worry.

Alix came through the surgery very well. She was still in a bit of pain for a while, but took it very stoically. During this time, of course, she could look forward to having the pain go away. If this had been put off, something would have developed in which she could only look forward to pain getting worse.

An additional item. A week before all that, I noticed that the ashtrays that Alix used had been unused for a few days. (She had been a pack-a-day smoker for 34 years.) She told me that she had quit because they would not let her smoke in the hospital. When I asked if she were trying to acclimate herself, she replied, 'Yeah, I'm in training.'

Perhaps I might like at this point to discuss some ramifications of Alix quitting smoking. This, of course, brings up the question of my pipe smoking. As a true-believer pipe smoker, I do not inhale. (I realize that another's such statement might call my credibility into question, but that's another story.) Pipe smokers avoid inhaling by a sucking action, similar to that used when drinking soda through a straw. The problem that I saw there is that this means that there would be a lot of second-hand smoke. What would normally go into my lungs goes into the air instead. I decided that I would not smoke in our apartment or near her when outdoors. This was made easy because of the fact that I do not inhale. I have never had an addiction, so I have not been plagued by nicotine fits. Thus, she quit and I cut back.

One benefit of pipe smoking is the pleasant aroma. I have gotten many compliments on the kind of tobacco that I use, especially from women. However, if that aroma ever got me into a woman's bedroom,

I am sure that the only thing that she would let me do is smoke my pipe.

I had realized (and many pointed this out to me) that the second-hand smoke from my pipe could not only be deleterious, but also might help trigger a dormant cigarette craving. If I were the only one involved, I could have been in denial to myself or defensive toward those others, but where Alix was concerned – no way! She very graciously suggested that a viable solution might be to run the blower continually on our central air conditioning, to use filters with electro-static particles, and to change the filter often. This didn't really solve the problem, so I now no longer smoke my pipe in our apartment, nor do I smoke elsewhere in her presence.

As I write this, I am not dislocating my shoulder from patting myself on the back. It was no big deal because, as I said, I did not smoke to satisfy a nicotine addiction, but for some oral gratification and something to do with my hands. I guess that one might call it a socially acceptable form of thumb-sucking.

This issue recently became important for reasons that were quite specific. Alix had been plagued by something of a chronic cough. Although her chest x-ray had shown nothing bad, I was worried and had her see a specialist in pulmonary diseases. He diagnosed her as having asthma, very likely going back to the years even before she started smoking. Thus, making these decisions about our smoking turned out to be quite prudent.

On Friday afternoon, 27 August, Alix's gynecologist told her that she could be turned loose on the following Saturday morning. (Perhaps 'turned loose' smacks a bit of incarceration, but hospitals and prisons do have one important thing in common. The first question people ask each other is, 'What are you in here for?') She was gaining strength and it was felt that she would no longer need to be closely watched. One hopeful circumstance was that, since the pathology report showed that the growths on the inside of the cervix were not invasive, there would be no need to look for malignancies elsewhere in her body as there was almost no chance of them coming back. Alix qualified the 'almost' by saying, 'There's no chance at all that they will come back on the parts that were removed.'

The report even uncovered the cause of her intermittent bleeding, something that had baffled the doctors. It seems they discovered that there was a large undiagnosed hemorrhagic cyst on an ovary (caused by drugs and the trauma of cut-and-release during the cone biopsy). That too was over and done with.

I came to get Alix on Saturday morning. The paperwork was completed, her belongings were gathered, and we departed. The doctor who signed the release order gave me a fistful of prescriptions and also a list of non-prescription items. After I dropped Alix off and assured myself that the situation was well in hand, I went to the pharmacy and got what was needed. Our two cats, being cats, gave no indication that they had noticed that anyone was away. However, Alix and I think that this is part of their charm.

When Alix was admitted, following surgery, I made one of my Black Forest cherry chocolate cakes. (I mentioned at the beginning of this book that one of my hobbies was gourmet cooking. Should anyone wonder how this jibes with my record of weight loss, note that I wrote 'gourmet cooking' not 'gourmet eating'.) I gave the cake to the nurses and told them that it was a totally shameless bribe for them to give her super extra care. I told them that if I got bad reports, I would make a second cake, but this time the batter would contain garlic powder, curry powder, and horseradish. Alix told me that she had a sufficient amount of tender loving care, so on Friday I made two loaves of my own recipe low-fat banana bread to give to the nurses on Saturday. (For the recipes, see Appendix A.)

Alix's recovery was very rapid, to the amazement of both her doctors and myself. She seemed to know exactly how to pace herself. From time to time, she would stop what she was doing and take a long nap. Alix was more than pleased with the care she got. The whole time, everything that could possibly go awry was carefully monitored by specialists and technicians. She even had good words for the clerical staff. To show her appreciation, she even set up a web site singing the praises of all of them, as well as of the hospital itself.

After Alix's release, she got a follow-up phone call from one of the hospital's public relations people, inquiring as to her satisfaction. I heard her rate everyone a '10'. As examples of her sense of humor, even under these trying circumstances, I also heard the answers that she gave (with her usual grin) to a couple of questions they must have asked her. Toward the start of the conversation, she said, 'I liked the outpatient surgery so much, I decided to come back two weeks later for some inpatient.' Toward the end, she said, 'Oh, yes, I'm going to have all of my hysterectomies done in that hospital.'

My second crisis

This could be called a cautionary tale. It shows that if one has led an unhealthy lifestyle, even if one has reformed, chickens might still be coming home to roost.

For a few years, about once or twice a year, I have had some pains that were at the time considered no cause for concern. They consisted of aches that started at about the solar plexus, went up into the neck and head, and out to the arms. On a scale of 1 to 10, they were a 1, and only lasted about a minute. They also had no throbbing. Add to that the fact that, at my annual physicals, my EKGs were perfect. As a result, I did not pay any attention to the pains, and chalked them up to indigestion or some such thing.

On Wednesday, 31 January 2001, I awoke at 3.00am, with that pain. (Since Alix works nights at her security guard job, she was not there.) It was now a 2 or 3 on the pain scale, but after about two minutes it went away so I felt relieved, and paid no attention to it. Being a short sleeper, I awoke for good at 4.00am. At 5.00am the pain came back at a level of 5 or so and lasted for five minutes, after which it went away again. At about 6.00am, I fixed myself some breakfast.

Then at 7.00am, the pain came back as an 8. I have a very high pain threshold, so if I were in such pain, anyone else would consider it excruciating. Somewhere between seven and ten minutes later, I started to break out into a sweat. At that point, I realized that it was something quite serious and dialed 911, the number used to report emergencies.

The paramedics came in record time and gave me a thorough look-over. My blood pressure was 220/110. By law, they are required to take one only to the nearest emergency facility. As luck would have it, it was about a quarter mile away and had a unit specializing in cardiac problems.

My lack of sensitivity to danger came into high relief when the paramedics arrived. To make sure that they got to the right place, I went outside our front door and waited for them. When the ambulance got there, I called to them, told them to come up, and followed them inside. After they were in my apartment, one of them asked me where the patient was. They were all astonished when I identified myself as the one they were looking for.

At the emergency room, an EKG showed that I had not had a heart attack. So what was it then? I was given a number of medicines, was admitted to the hospital, and was assigned a cardiologist. He told me that the normal EKG showed that I had not had a heart attack, but that this did not mean that I was out of the woods. He then said that he wanted to do a stress test on me, and that this would indicate whether or not there was any heart trouble involved. If not, he said that acid reflux could cause the pain that I had experienced and that this could be controlled by medication. This surprised me, because I thought that the acid reflux problem had cured itself when I lost all of that weight. He told me that a stress test would be scheduled for the following day. Among other questions, he asked me if I had exercised regularly. I told him that because of a history of asthma, I could not work out with weights or jog, and had relied instead on doing a lot of walking. His facial expression said, 'Yeah, sure. That's what all the couch potatoes say.'

The next day I did the stress test. For those unfamiliar with this, you walk on a treadmill, with speed increasing, until the heartbeat rate exceeds 100 per minute. Then, high-tech scans are done of your heart, with more scans done after three hours of rest. This tells the cardiologist how your heart is doing. There was a bit of humor in this. The treadmill had to be speeded up quite a bit before the 100 beats per minute threshold was reached. During this the doctor said, 'You must walk a lot.' I replied, 'I told you yesterday that I did.' He then said, 'Now I believe you.'

The results of the stress test showed that a portion of my heart was not getting the blood it needed. So much for something as simple as acid reflux! The next step was to determine what was causing this. This was done by an angiogram, where a catheter is inserted into a vein via an incision near the groin and is pushed into the heart, showing if there is a blockage and if so, what kind. At worst, they could discover that open-heart surgery was needed at once.

This was not the case. A blockage was found in the right coronary artery that could be opened by balloon angioplasty, which as the name implies, opens the blockage by inflating a balloon. The procedure was successful and a stainless steel tube, called a stint, was put in place to make the newly freed artery hold its shape. Another stress test is done a few months later, to find out if there is any lasting heart damage. I am quite hopeful. Ironically, if there is no such damage, then my heart will be in better shape than it was before this incident. At worst, it will be no worse.

During this procedure, I was given what is called an interruptible sedative that would enable me to be awakened if need be, but would allow me to fall back asleep. When the doctor came in, after a team of four technicians had readied the site, he woke me up to say 'Hello.' I could not go back to sleep, and was awake for the entire procedure. I found it quite fascinating, in particular the coordination of the doctor-technicians team, and the kind of orders the doctor gave. In particular, I was intrigued by the orders to inflate the balloon. The duration was given in seconds, but the strength was given in 'atmospheres'.

As an aside, as I have mentioned, Alix works as a security guard. She was assigned to the 11.00pm to 7.00am shift, so she would stop by to see me on the way home from work. The nurses and other staff people could not get over how, given the seriousness of the circumstances, we joked around so much but then they did not know who and what we are. On Thursday morning, after I told her what the possible outcomes were, she said, 'If I catch you ignoring what the doctors tell you to do...', and with her usual grin, she reached into her equipment belt and held up a pair of handcuffs.

At the end of the procedure the doctor, knowing that I had been conscious throughout, asked me about any pain and discomfort that I may have undergone. I replied that the only really painful parts were in the beginning, when a urination catheter was inserted, and during the procedure, when the balloon was inflated. Everything else could come under the heading of discomfort. After he left, I asked one of the technicians what happened to people with my problem before this technology was invented. He replied that they would go on to suffer one or more heart attacks, one of which was sure to kill them. I told him, 'There is your cost-benefit analysis.'

There was an amusing end to this incident. It happened just before my discharge from the hospital. In order to appreciate it, I have to tell about a very good friend of Alix and me.

This person is a retired major of the US Army, had enlisted as a private and rose up through the ranks, was a paratrooper (during both enlisted and commissioned service), is a Gulf War veteran and, as a result of that service, has three life-threatening conditions: hypertension, Type I diabetes, and hepatitis C. I cannot tell you what his name is. Why? Because *her* name is Gloria.

Gloria lives in North Carolina near Fort Bragg, the home base of the 82nd Airborne Division. She was with that unit, except for the time when she was in the Persian Gulf and the year when she was a Signal Corps company commander in Korea.

After my angioplasty, I was taken to the intensive care unit (ICU), where I stayed until my discharge the following morning. Shortly after I finished eating breakfast, one of the nurses came into my room with a perplexed expression on her face. She said, 'Someone just called you from out-of-state. She said that your wife had given her this number, and that she is your girlfriend.' (Rooms in the ICU have no phones.) I thought to myself, 'What? Who?' Suddenly lights started flashing and bells started ringing. I asked the nurse, 'Was that other state North

Carolina?' 'Yes it was,' she replied. 'Oh, God,' I said, 'That has to be Gloria.' It was; Alix confirmed it when she came to check me out and take me home. I had to leave the nurse in her bewildered state, because this was one of those circumstances where the more you try to explain the worse it sounds.

To tie together any loose ends of this incident, on 10 August I was given the second stress test that I mentioned earlier. I was given a clean bill of health. Before this, my cardiologist had talked of a program of cardiac rehabilitation and the taking of a number of medications until I should die of something else. None of that. All that is needed are periodic check-ups. This confirmed my contention that this was certainly those chickens coming home to roost from those six years when I had an unhealthy lifestyle. In fact, with that coronary artery blockage gone, my heart is in better condition than it was before this happened.

Some Thoughts on Theological Topics

I gave a somewhat detailed account of my religious beliefs in my auto-biography,[30] discussing both the reasons, and the obstacles I had to overcome, for my being an adult convert to Roman Catholicism. This was totally the result of study and reflection. Briefly, I had sought a firm philosophical foundation for my ideas on social and economic justice.

Given my tendency to see and evaluate things from an unconventional standpoint, my theological viewpoint was no exception. While orthodox, my interpretations do tend to the atypical.

One God? Why not many?

That is a good question, isn't it? Since we live in a society whose dominant religions are the three monotheistic religions (Christianity, Judaism, and Islam, especially the first), we take it for granted that there is only one God, and relegate a belief in a plethora of gods to mythology. To answer this, we need to ask, 'What is a god?'

To many, even in our society, we think of a supernatural being that controls the forces of nature. After all, we pray for rain, cessation of too much rain, hot weather, cool weather, safety from storms and earthquakes, and so on. The prayers generally imply that natural disasters are things that might be our fault, and the applicable god must be placated by one means or another. However, if this is the case, why is there not a god for each situation that is involved? Isn't this simply specialization? Taking it this way, when the ancient Jews announced to the world that there was only one god, this could be interpreted as saying that God was a generalist rather than a specialist.

To answer that, one must look at an interesting thing about polytheistic religions: in those belief systems there was existence before these gods came upon the scene. In Greek mythology, the gods were the children of the Titans, who were overthrown by Zeus. In Norse mythology, the gods were preceded by the frost giants and trolls, who themselves were spontaneously generated from a great pit between frost and fire.

The notion that the Jews introduced to human thought was that, what they called 'God', was the source of all being, which thus could have no antecedents. When I told this concept to Shari Lynn, a friend, who is a 31-year-old high-functioning autistic woman who had become so as a result of an automobile accident, and who had adopted orthodox Judaism, she replied, 'Then sin could be considered as something that goes against the nature of being.' (This bit of insightful thinking could be considered as a good example of the perceptiveness of the autistic.) By the nature of such a thing, there could be only one God, yet most people do encounter a great deal of difficulty in grasping such a concept. This leads to anthropomorphization or the ascribing to God of human characteristics, which leads to the remark, attributed to any number of anti-religious individuals, that God created people in His own image, and people returned the compliment. While wry and amusing, this should not be allowed to preclude understanding and acceptance of this idea.

I have, on this topic, spent some amount of space on the fact that a belief in a single God, as the source of all being, was the major contribution to world culture of the Jews. There is no small amount of irony in the fact that the other religions most dependent on that concept, Christianity and Islam, have contained more than their fair share of Jew-haters. This irony was most fittingly expressed by some graffiti that I once saw. It was my favorite kind of graffiti, in that someone had written a response underneath it. It went:

> How odd of God
> To choose the Jews.

The response was:

> But not as odd
> As those who choose
> A Jewish God,
> Yet spurn the Jews.

Worshiping the Devil

Stories in the media, both mainstream and 'other', abound with coteries (and individuals) that worship the Devil. In addition to real groups, this is the subject of just about all horror movies or books (good, bad, or indifferent).

The Devil is, in this context, a malevolent supernatural being, with many such followers. In the Christian tradition, both from the Book of Revelation and John Milton's epic *Paradise Lost*, he is one of the highest-ranking of all angels. (His name, Lucifer, is Latin for 'the light bearer'.) Driven by pride, the worst of the seven deadly sins, he believed that he should be the equal of God and convinced many other angels that he could do likewise for them. They all suffered the fate of eternal separation from God since they had, in effect, separated themselves.

In the fictitious versions, people are essentially powerless against these evil forces. The only way they can be defeated, and usually are, is by a very clever human person 'beating the devil at his own game'.

This 'hero' would have to be an actual or potential victim. There can be no mention of any possibility of a beneficent supernatural force as a foil for the Devil. This would tend to reduce those victims to bystanders in such a battle, which makes for very poor drama because this would give these victims nothing to fear.

Also, if we allow for a benevolent supernatural force, then we are not powerless against the Devil. He can do nothing to us without our total cooperation. The only power he can have over us is the power we give him.

Victimhood is not essential, because devil-worshipers are not victims of the Devil (at least not unwilling ones) but, one could say, confederates. There are cases in fiction where there is a formal pact involved for the hope of specific benefits to be received. The quintessential literary example is that of Faust.

What of the real-life devil-worshiping groups? People are usually aghast when they learn of their existence nearby. Tales become rampant about such things as baby sacrifice even though, in all cases, any subsequent investigation fails to discover any evidence of that. Perhaps these fears are fed by the fictitious versions.

Occasionally one does read of a brutal serial killer who, when captured, says he or she did it as a way of worshiping the Devil. His or her victims are sacrificial offerings. These are invariably individual pathologies and are not found in any of these groups. (If the 'Devil' were not the catalyst for their acts, something else would suffice.) The latter are generally harmless people who satisfy their need for social bonding by 'strange' rites, ceremonial garments, and unintelligible chants, and whose egos seem to be boosted by the extent to which they shock others. Those who find what they do to be distasteful would do well simply to ignore them. Paradoxically, what they do could be considered to be a backhanded endorsement of religion. As the old saying goes, 'if there is a Devil, surely there must be a God?'

I had heard of such groups when I was growing up in New York City. There were two practices of theirs that I found singularly amusing. One was that a person would go to Mass and communion, put in his or her mouth a desiccant to prevent the wafer from dissolving, and bring it back to the group, where it would be made an offering to the Devil. In the other case, a 'black Mass' would consist of a defrocked priest copulating with a virgin on an altar to the Devil, her virginity being such an offering. This was a rarely performed ritual for a funny reason. While there were in the big city, unfrocked priests aplenty, genuine virgins were quite hard to come by.

Does this mean that true Devil worship exists only in fancy? Hardly. If this is the case, how does it manifest itself? Not by the practices I have described, which either horrify or amuse people. These are not the sort of things that would seduce many 'reasonable' people, and make them want to willingly turn over their souls to the Devil.

To see how this is done, we have to go to the fourth chapter of Matthew's gospel. Between Jesus' baptism, and prior to the start of his ministry (with the Sermon on the Mount), He spent 40 days in the desert, where three times he was tempted by the Devil. It is the third temptation that is crucial. The Devil showed him the wealth and splendor of all the kingdoms of the world and told him, 'I will give you all of these, if you will prostrate yourself and worship me.' The evangelist reports that the Devil was unable to get Jesus to acquiesce.

I wrote above that for the Devil to have any power over us, we have to give him that power. For this, there need be neither rituals nor any incantations. All we have to do is adopt the Devil's values.

The gospel passage to which I referred shows how to do that. In place of 'the kingdoms of the world,' read 'a custom house with a designer interior in an upscale neighborhood, one's children in exclusive private schools, membership in one or more country clubs, things in your house and your driveway to make others jealous, and something big tied up to your dock'. The Devil will promise you those and other such things if you will worship him. One does not even need to physically prostrate oneself, all that one need do is to come to believe that these are the kind of things that are the most important in life and that one should do whatever it takes to obtain them. From that point on, no matter one's explicit awareness of it, one is worshiping the Devil. Can the Devil really always deliver on this? Hardly. In the Catholic baptism ritual, one promises to reject the Devil 'and all his empty promises'. Even if these things are not obtained, it is believing that they are the most important life goals that is the pivotal decision.

I might note that, in the Chapter of Matthew that follows Jesus' temptations by the Devil, he begins his earthly ministry with the Sermon on the Mount, which begins with the Beatitudes. The first of these is: 'Blessed are the poor in spirit.' This means that, even if you are the CEO of a Fortune 500 company, you should not live much more opulently than the majority of your employees.

Why God puts people to the test

According to the Biblical story,[31] God tested Abraham by ordering him to sacrifice Isaac, his son, but stopped him before the boy was actually killed. Abraham was then told that since he had passed the test, there would be great rewards for him.

Every time I ask someone why God needed to put Abraham to such a draconian test, I get the answer that God wanted to know if Abraham would obey His orders without question. Stop and think about this. God did not know? What about omniscience? The fact is, God knew exactly how Abraham would react. However, God also knew that it was important for Abraham to know what his reaction would be in such a circumstance. God had big plans for Abraham, and realized that if Abraham knew that he would not shrink from such an unreasonable command as this, he would be up to any of the future reasonable ones.

I look upon my own trials in a similar light. As I have survived each of them, I have come out of it with a new capability that I did not realize that I had. This goes to the final lines, written by Gustav Mahler, for the closing of his monumental Second Symphony: 'Was du geschlagen: Zu Gott wird es dich tragen!' which translates as: 'That with which you have struggled: It will carry you to God!'

How could God be so cruel to his own son?

I have often been asked, both by non-Christians, by ex-Christians, and especially by anti-Christians (a subset of those who are anti all religions), why a loving, kind, and merciful God would require His son to go through such excruciating agony in order to redeem people from the consequences of their misdeeds. Isn't this overkill − literally? Could God not have simply decreed this, and called a prophet to announce it to people? (The word 'prophet' is to be taken in its literal sense: a messenger, and not in the popular sense: a seer.)

Indeed, one must consider the events in the Christian liturgical calendar in which the events effecting redemption (prior to the resurrection) are celebrated: the entry into Jerusalem, the betrayal, the last supper, the crucifixion, and the burial. They are called *Passiontide*, which comes from *passio*, the Latin word for 'suffering'.

One must consider also that, at least in my experience, these critics are not malicious, but are mostly well-meaning. They hate to see anyone suffer, especially needlessly. They argue that this tends to show in God a rather sadistic streak, which would belie the notion of God as being the epitome of kindness and mercy. Given this, why does Christianity cling to this notion? The most common symbol of Christianity is the cross, symbolizing the crucifixion, easily the most inhumane method of execution. (Even burning at the stake is relatively mild, being all over and done with in a couple of minutes.) One may as well imagine a religion adopting as its symbol a gallows, a guillotine, or an electric chair.

Perhaps this is a good place to define just what is meant by 're-demption'. Because of people's misdeeds, they had separated themselves from God − the source of all being. Even their good works were insufficient to 'even the score'. Redemption meant that henceforth people would be able, by their deeds, to earn salvation, an eternal direct relationship with God.

Christians argue that God did it through such suffering to show the depth of His love for His people.[32] It effected God's second great act of love for His people, the first being creation. Nevertheless, given the alternative method mentioned above, does this not beg the critics'

question: did God need to use such a draconian method? I believe that
the answer lies in how humans attach any credibility to love.

'Love' is a major topic in all forms of art. (I am ignoring any
modern usage, which might use 'making love' as a euphemism for a
one night stand with a total stranger, for self-gratification only.) While
painting and music are certainly included in this, it is in literature that
one sees how people make expressions of love, which since it is totally
inwardly experienced, gives the only insight as to how one might be
able to recognize it in another person.

Since the world is full of phonies, seducers, chiselers, and cheaters,
the question of the sincerity of this expression is of no mean consequence. There must be some recognizable standard of credibility that
people need to use in order to gauge not only the existence of that sincerity, but also its depth.

With very few exceptions, if one examines love poetry, love songs,
romantic stories, and so on, the one standard of credibility for love that
people seem willing to accept is willingness to suffer. If the suffering
becomes actual, then that is considered proof positive of love. Among
the very few notable exceptions are Shakespeare's 29th sonnet and
Schumann's song *Widmung*. In particular, it is the poem by Friedrich
Rü ckert, used by Schumann as the text for his song (for the texts of
these, see appendices B and C).

A hypothetical case in point would be a woman who is being
courted by two men and is interested in neither; each of the two men
cares for her equally. (The same example would be true if the genders
were reversed.) Being a decent sort and not wishing to gratify her ego
by stringing them along, she tells them both that she is not interested.
(Remember that I said that this example was hypothetical.)

One man, desiring her happiness and not wanting to make her
uncomfortable by continuing to press his suit, wishes her well and
then bows out of her life gracefully, privately nursing any hurts he
might have. The other gives vent to paroxysms of anguish, pleads with
her not to condemn him to a life of loneliness, begs their mutual
friends to intercede for him, and perhaps starts drinking or indulging
in other forms of self-destructive behavior.

One hardly need ask which of them the woman will believe loved her the more. The second one, of course, because he seemingly suffered the most as a result of being deprived of any reciprocation on her part.

This defies all logic. One would think that love is of a nature that would desire the happiness of the object of that love, even if it is unrequited. Nevertheless, it is as they say, 'human nature' (albeit, to say the least, one of its less admirable aspects).

Given this, if God had chosen another method of informing people of their redemption (such as I mentioned before), what would have been the reaction on the part of people? I suspect that it would have varied from at best, a shrug of the shoulders and saying something to the effect of, 'How nice,' to at worst, totally ignoring it and going about 'more important matters'. The current state of the earth's ecology is witness to how seriously humans take creation, God's first act of love, which was accompanied by no observable suffering.

Therefore, for this greatest of gifts of love to be credible, there had to be the greatest suffering on the part of the greatest: God Himself. To bring this to pass, God had to take on human form, resulting in another important event in the Christian liturgical calendar: the incarnation.

It can thus be seen that the depth of God's love was not so much that He underwent such agony to redeem humanity but that, in doing so, He was willing to accommodate and indulge one of its less exemplary idiosyncrasies.

Judgement

One thing that I like about Pushkin[33] is that he does not allow his villains the easy closure of death. They have to live with the consequences of what they have done. Gherman, in Pikovaya Dama (The Queen of Spades), does not (as he does in Tchaikovsky's operatic adaptation) kill himself, but goes insane, and spends the rest of his life in an asylum, flipping the three imaginary cards that were supposed to bring him fortune.

The same is true for Yevgeny Onegin. (Here, the Pushkin work and the Tchaikovsky opera end the same way.) Years before the end, he spurned the love of Tatiana, a young girl of the rural nobility, because, while he found her attractive, marriage to her would cramp his bohemian lifestyle. He also humiliates her with a moral lecture on 'throwing herself' at him. At the end, after he had traveled far and wide (having killed his best friend in a senseless duel), he returns lonely, bored, and feeling useless. At a party in which he hopes to alleviate his boredom, he again sees Tatiana, who is now married to the host, a high-ranking nobleman, government official, and former general. She has bloomed into a refined woman of the world while retaining the genuineness of her youth. (Her husband tells Onegin that on meeting her, being surrounded all day by poseurs and sycophants, she was like the proverbial breath of fresh air.) Onegin is taken with her immediately, and begs her to leave her husband and go away with him. Reminding him of how, long ago, he so curtly dismissed her love, she also tells him that while she still has some feelings for him, in no way is she going to desert her husband. She then walks away, telling him never to contact her again. He is left in despair, facing an empty and lonely life.

Consider Onegin's state at the end. He realizes that he now sees what could have made his life rich, full, and rewarding. He realizes that he has lost that forever. He also realizes that it was the result of choices that he alone had made. Isn't this what condemnation to hell must be like?

Many reports of out-of-body experiences, following clinical death, have told of being approached by a 'light presence' (likely an angel), who showed the person scenes from his life, and asked him to evaluate them. This is significant. Hell is not a place of physical torment, but a state of being in which one is totally and eternally isolated from the source of all being. By reviewing one's life, one is made to realize that this is a self-isolation caused by the choices one has made. God does not condemn anyone to hell; they condemn themselves. This is opposed to a popular view in which God is portrayed like Beckmesser, in Wagner's opera *Die Meistersinger*, who determines membership worthiness in the guild by marking down the applicant's faults as he hears them. After exceeding a certain number, the applicant is deemed unfit, and is rejected.

The phrase 'fear of God' is not unrelated to the ideas about judgement. It is mentioned often in the Bible, and is part of our culture. When we talk of making someone obey the law, we talk of 'putting the fear of God into him (or her)'. It is necessary to see just what is said in the scriptures. It must be remembered that they were written in Hebrew and in Greek.

In the New Testament, the word that is used is *phobos*. This word means, not a terror type of fear, but an awe that comes from a healthy respect for the nature of things. Incidentally, it is my understanding that, in the Hebrew scriptures, the corresponding word has the same connotation. (It is ironic that the suffix *phobia* has come to mean fears that are irrational, e.g. claustrophobia, etc.) It is the sort of fear that causes us to not stick an ice pick into an electrical outlet or to go outside in a thunderstorm.

It was mentioned earlier that an adverse final judgement results from doing things analogous to this, to do things against the nature of being. That being the case, why is this phrase so often interpreted in terms of terror at God's displeasure? I believe that it comes from the cozy church-state relationship that started with the Roman Emperor Theodosius I (who ruled from 347–395, and made Christianity the state religion of the Roman Empire) and which did not end until fairly recently. The displeasure that was to strike terror in to people was not God's, but that of the ruler.

Fundamentalism and religion

I often find myself caught between two extremes on this issue. On the one hand, there are the anti-religious people, who look at passages in the Bible that go against scientific knowledge (I am not thinking of scientific hypotheses, but of clearly observable phenomena), and use that to conclude that religion is equivalent to superstition. On the other hand, there are those religionists who, looking at the Bible as

God's inspired word, insist that it must be interpreted literally, even if that defies reason or things that are clearly observable. The best of this is that they do not study the original Hebrew or Greek but some commonly available English translation.

I am not a member of either camp. Because of my background in physics, I am convinced that the universe had to have a beginning, and as such, a creator. This ultimately is the supernatural source of all being. Still, this does not compel me to accept things that defy my perception and experience. How do I reconcile this?

The key word is 'inspired', which is not the same as 'dictated'. God, to send a message to people, put ideas into the minds of the writers of the books of the Bible, who then wrote that message, but expressed through their own perceptions and experiences. (This is an example of how I believe God acts: working for people through other people.) It is the job of the Biblical scholar to filter those out. As a result, much of holy scripture can be considered allegory, an approach used by many great writers to make a point. I should like to stress the word 'dictate' because, in the tradition of Islam, the archangel Gabriel appeared to Mohammed (who is believed by many to have been illiterate), and dictated the Quran to him, word for word. No such thing exists in the Judeo-Christian tradition. Yet Averroes, the 12th century Islamic philosopher who, therefore, had considerably less room for maneuver than Jews or Christians, wrote that if a passage in the Quran appears to contradict fact or reason, then there must be an interpretation other than the literal. For those unfamiliar with Averroes, his real name was Ibn Rushd, which Christian Spaniards had great difficulty in pronouncing. He wrote many commentaries on Aristotle, which influenced such diverse theologians as St Thomas Aquinas and Moses Maimonides.

As examples of such contradictions, I should like to refer to the first and last books of the Bible. In Genesis 1: 14–18 the sun is created on the fourth day. Since a day is defined as the time between two successive appearances of the sun in the sky, how could days be counted before there was a sun? In Revelation 12: 4, a dragon swept his tail over the sky, and a third of the stars were knocked loose and fell to the earth. Knowing what we now know about what and where the stars are, this is impossible. These have to be allegorical images. For what? What are the messages?

The basic message in Genesis 1 is that God, being the source of all being, created all things. The writer used his limited knowledge of cosmology to create a story to make that point. The basic message in Revelation is that Christ will come again into the world. Everything else is an allegorical description reflecting the author's view of the moral corruption of the Roman Empire, even at the height of its power. (Traditionally, this author is held to be the apostle John, but many consider this to be doubtful.) In that sense, it is a very subversive book so the author had to use allegory to keep from running afoul of the law. Quite possibly, had the author's knowledge of astronomy been more comprehensive, he might have used other symbolism.

My favorite example of the use of allegory is the story of Adam and Eve and the forbidden fruit, given in Genesis 3. Since scientific knowledge goes counter to the story of creation, as given literally, what is the message contained therein? First, the name of the tree whose fruit was forbidden to the first humans was 'the knowledge of good and evil'. (I am amazed at how many, believer and non-believer alike, are ignorant of this.) The consequence of eating the fruit of this tree was death. What of all that? Suppose we consider our primordial ancestors. In the course of their evolutionary development they came to understand the difference between good and evil and acquired the ability to make a choice between them. Before that they were in a protected state (like the garden of Eden?), in that they could not be held responsible for such choices. After that, they no longer enjoyed such protection because they were accountable for the choices they made (the expulsion?) and would have to suffer any results that came if they chose against God. The ultimate consequence would be eternal separation from God, which could be called a spiritual form of death.

A scientific discovery that I would like to discuss is the one which, among many religionists, is the most emotionally charged of all: evolution. Those who attack it insist that any who support it must, of need, deny the truth of the Bible. They say that scripture plainly says that humans were created in God's image.[34] To take this literally, i.e. that people look like God implies, by the mathematical principle of reflexivity, that God looks like the people He created. This gives rise to a number of interesting questions. Is God more than six feet tall? Does He have red hair? Is He white? Is He a he?

These questions sound ridiculous and they are, unless you take the Genesis quotation strictly by itself, in which case they become quite serious. However, there is another Biblical reference which shows that the Bible can be squared with the idea of evolution without contorting either.

It says in the gospels that God is a spirit.[35] As such, He does not possess a body, rendering all of those questions at best irrelevant. Those passages from Genesis and John's Gospel, taken together, lead to what is (for me anyhow) the inescapable conclusion that it was not the human body that was created in God's image, but the human soul. There is absolutely nothing in the Bible that says that the human body could not have evolved from other forms of life. The first humans were a mutation of some other species. At some point in time, God imbued them with the immortal soul that was like Him.

It thus appears that an acceptance of the idea of biological evolution can go a long way toward giving a person a substantial appreciation of just exactly what part of himself it is that has the spark of divinity.

Having or changing a religion

How do I see religion? It is a system of ethics and metaphysics that presupposes a supernatural source. (There is an alternate view that I will discuss later.) One key to this question was given by a philosophy professor I had as a college undergraduate some decades back, who said, 'Everyone has metaphysics and an ethics even if they can neither spell nor pronounce those words.'

These things can be explained in detail with clarity but alas, not with brevity. I will say that metaphysics is a way of looking at the world and one's place in it, while ethics is a way of determining how one interacts with others. (For a more detailed explanation, see Appendix D.)

Thus, it turns out that atheism, agnosticism, secularism, and amorphous religions, as well as religions with defined theologies, are all special cases of the broader category of metaphysical and ethical systems. Each in its own way represents the way each person sees himself as fitting into the world he comprehends, and the way in which he interacts with other people.

Unless a person is totally wishy-washy, he should only be willing to change these bedrock beliefs if he is given sufficient evidence that they are wrong, since they are not like a garment that can be painlessly removed and changed for another, but are part and parcel of what makes him what he is. This could be said to be the person's *essence*. Under no circumstances should he be asked to change just to please someone else. The statement (all too often uttered in the case in which two people have different sets of beliefs), 'You are putting your religion ahead of our relationship,' has no more validity or fairness than does, 'You are putting your unbelief ahead of our relationship.'

This brings us to that other view of what is a religion, i.e. a tradition that comes from one's family, ethnic, or national background. While a religion defined by a set of metaphysical and ethical positions is one that is something belonging uniquely to an individual (that it might also be shared by others is irrelevant here), one based on family, ethnic, or national background is determined by the circumstances one is born into. This gives rise to the expression, 'I/you/he/she was born a...' I find this at best misleading. Every newborn baby is an agnostic, in the literal sense of that word – from the Greek for 'without knowledge'. This type of 'religion' gives rise to two problems.

One is that, unless the person actually comes to believe in the metaphysics and ethics of his imposed religion, then that person is, as they say, 'going through the motions'. The person's ethics might actually be quite at variance with the teachings of that faith, which tends to put that faith in quite a bad light when the person's actions are viewed by others.

The second goes to a mantra of the anti-religious: how much evil has been done in the name of religion. I cannot think of any such atrocity – from torture and killing to ostracizing – in which fealty to a particular religion was not used as a measure for family, ethnic, or national loyalty, which makes it not religion, but chauvinism. Of course, one can also bear in mind the agonies visited in the name of 'love'. Also, consider the last words of the Girondist Mme Roland, as she was about to be executed by the guillotine: 'O liberty, what crimes they commit in your name.'

This is not to trivialize such loyalties. They represent one's ties to one's ancestral heritage, which to most people constitutes no small amount of their feeling of personal identity. There is a story that I believe epitomizes the persistence of ethnicity.

> I grew up in New York City. At the time, there were two types of law firms. There were the midtown firms, serving the corporate and financial worlds. They had WASP-y names like Cravath, Swain, and Moore. Then there were the downtown firms, clustered around City Hall and the criminal courts building. They had names that reflected the ethnic makeup of the city at the time: Jewish, Italian, and Irish. One such firm was named Cohen, Giordano, and Mulvaney. One day Cohen came in late and told his colleagues, 'I'm the fourth generation of my family in this country, and I thought that it was time to assimilate. So this morning I stopped at the courthouse and had my name legally changed to Smith.' The other two attorneys nodded in acquiescence. A couple of days later, Giordano came in late and told the others, 'I had to agree with our partner. So this morning I also had my name changed to Smith.' About a week later, Mulvaney told the others that, having seen the wisdom of what they did he decided to do likewise, and that legally, he was now named Smith. They took down the old shingle that said 'Cohen, Giordano, and Mulvaney,' and put up a new one that said 'Smith, Smith, and Smith.' The next morning, the telephone rang, and the receptionist answered, 'Good morning. Smith, Smith, and Smith, attorneys at law. May I help you?' 'Yes,' the caller said, 'I'd like

to speak to Mr. Smith.' 'Certainly, sir,' the receptionist replied, 'Which Mr. Smith would you like to speak to: Cohen, Giordano, or Mulvaney?'

However, to me this is not a religion, and I wish that people would draw upon another word or phrase for it. I use the word 'loyalty' because, when a person changes his or her religion for philosophical reasons others, for whom it is a group identity thing, treat it as if it were a form of treason. If one looks upon religion in its philosophical sense, Polonius' admonition to his son, Laertes is quite applicable: 'This above all: to thine own self be true.'[36]

What about a 'mixed' marriage, i.e. a marriage in which the two parties have different religions? Is there a problem that could prove insurmountable? It depends upon in which sense one talks of religion. If the two people's religions stem from ethnic or national background, then I see no problem because it is a very good opportunity to expand the cultural horizons of both parties. Paradoxically, it is in this context that one or both families often insist that the other convert. But if the religions have a philosophical basis, then there could be trouble because this would, sooner or later, involve a clash of values. This would be compounded if the question were to come up about which values should be imparted to any children they might have.

Summing up these two understandings of religion, the one that comes from loyalty to a group and the other that comes from the way one sees the world, the former is a label placed on a person from the outside, while the latter is an integral part of the person's essence. (Even such a label need not be indelible. In the movie *Breaking Away*, a young man of a midwestern WASP family, for aesthetic reasons, decides to act as though his heritage were Italian.) I believe that it was in this sense, i.e. the way that one sees the world, that the United Nations' Declaration of Human Rights affirmed the right of each person to have a religion and also to change that religion.

Some Thoughts
on Political Topics

I have mentioned in my autobiography[37] that, as far back as I can remember, I have felt like an outsider. One consequence of this was that I identified with those that I perceived as outsiders. (These, in some circumstances, could even locally be the numerical majority.) This resulted in an awareness of social, political, and economic issues that started at about the age of 12.

This had even led to activism. In my high school yearbook (which came out in the fall of 1949), a black classmate wrote an inscription which said, in part, 'May we meet again in our fight for equality.' In my adolescent naivety, I thought that those who were for the things that I was for, did so for reasons similar to mine. Later I realized that many of them were only interested in highlighting our nation's shortcomings so that, before the world, Stalin would look good by comparison. Shortly after graduation from college, I was drafted into the Army. When I wanted to become an officer, these associations would come back to haunt me. There was a happy ending; I was commissioned after much explaining, which in retrospect was quite justified. Yet in getting rid of my illusions, I managed to retain my ideals. When asked to categorize my own political beliefs, I hesitate to call myself a liberal because I must then explain the difference between the liberalism of my youth and that of the trendy dilettantes who, since the mid-1960s, have been giving liberalism a bad name. I have come to tell people that it's a toss-up between the religious left and the radical center. Perhaps I can illustrate with some examples.

Democracy

I will start by making a statement that many will find surprising, if not shocking: democracy is not the normal form of government. The normal variety is for those self-promoting persons who are able to seize power and hold it, to do so. They can hold it almost indefinitely if they manage, for all others, to create a way of life that enables them to function in relative comfort by doing their jobs and keeping their mouths shut. There will always be dissidents who bewail the absence of some personal freedoms, but in situations such as these, they will be dismissed by most as irrelevant.

The only way for democracy to survive, let alone flourish, is for the citizenry to believe that the government is truly responsive to their concerns. Along with this there must be a widely-held belief that all have equal access to such a government.

When it is perceived by the citizenry that, in regards to this access, some are more equal than others, then democracy is in deep trouble. Good government, like justice, must not only be done, it must be seen to be done.

Locally, when a company with ties to local officials gets a lucrative contract to fix potholes in the streets, but the potholes remain, then this perception is damaged. The damage can be compounded if an election results in a change in the officials but this only results in a change in those who are favored. The same problem could exist on a national level, which is even worse because, in that case, the people feel even more powerless. This could even affect the national defense because people might begin to question whether we have a country that is worth defending.

During the time of the Weimar Republic, until the elections of 1932, the two leading parties in the Reichstag (the name of the elected legislative body) were the Socialists and the Centrists, the former moderately liberal and the latter moderately conservative. In the election of 1933, the two leading parties were the Nazis and the Communists. It would not take much deepening cynicism on the part of the public for something similar to happen in any democracy.

The rise and fall of civilizations

In the year 410 AD, the Visigoths, under their king Alaric, sacked Rome. They were a Germanic tribe that later conquered all of the Iberian peninsula after the collapse of the western Roman Empire, and ruled there until the Islamic incursion. It was not a surprise attack. The Romans knew when they had crossed the Danube and had followed their movement all the way but found themselves powerless to stop them. The Romans were dumbfounded. How could this happen? Was not Rome supposed to be invincible? Did they not have undisputed rule over the known world that anyone cared about? Was not Rome's primacy part of the natural order of things?

While the Roman population had been primarily Christian since the time of Constantine, there was still a sizeable pagan minority. Their leaders blamed it all on Christianity. They said that Rome had flourished when the old gods were worshiped, and that these gods protected Rome against such disasters. They said that under Christianity, the people had gotten soft, that they talked of things like peace and love, and that the young men would not serve in the army. They called for a return to the worship of the old gods, and to the virtues that they personified, the virtues that made Rome great. (Does this not sound familiar?)

The Christians turned to their most prominent intellectual spokesman, St Augustine for a reply. He was an adult convert who lived from 354 to 430. In addition to being a major Christian theologian, he was also Bishop of Hippo, a city in North Africa. The book he wrote as a reply was *The City of God*. This book, while written as an *ad hoc* rebuttal to the pagans, has very weighty implications for our own culture in our own time.

This book is in two parts. In the first part, St Augustine catalogues the calamities that befell Rome back in the days when the old gods were worshiped. The implication was that if they were supposed to have protected Rome, they did a very poor job of it.

In the second part he contrasts the City of God where the primary motivation is love, with the Human City where the primary motivation is greed. The former is motivated by the greatest of virtues, while the latter is motivated by the second worst of the seven deadly sins. His comments on the Human City are germane to the topic of what causes great powers first to rise to power and prosperity, but eventually to decay and collapse.

During the 'rise' phase, people's greed has a way of being constructive in its consequences. The desire to enrich oneself motivates people into ventures that increase production of goods and services, leading to strength for the nation, and prosperity for most, with the creation of employment opportunities that are better, both in quantity and quality. This also leads to a realistic belief on the part of the population that each person has a stake in the continued existence of that society and that their lives would be the worse if it were to collapse. As such, they are willing to make sacrifices for its preservation.

However, the fundamental motive on each person's part is personal gain and not the common good. Thus, great powers are built not on virtues, but on vices. But because it all pays off in what can be called 'the coin of this world,' the vices are mistaken for virtues. This leads to an attitude of attributing the 'success' of the Human City to the endorsement of whatever supernatural powers that be, including the methods that were used in gaining that success. (It could be argued that this amounts to pride – the worst of the seven deadly sins.)

Inevitably, however, a point of saturation is reached and there is no place for people's greed to be directed, except at each other. In this instance, when some people are enriched there is no corresponding increase in productivity and there may actually be a decline. Most people, who do not share in that enrichment and may even have their circumstances worsen, no longer feel that they have a stake in the society's survival and that any sacrifices that they make serve only for the enrichment of others, usually a privileged few. This is the 'fall' phase.

St Augustine stated that the fall could be averted if people were to substitute love for greed as their primary motivation and act accordingly. He did not believe this would happen, because of original sin. He summed things up by writing: 'The City of God lasts forever, while the greatest city in the world lies in ruins.' This is essentially a synopsis of St Augustine's thesis, writing about Rome in the 5th century. I should like to add a few observations of my own as they pertain to our country in today's world.

An example of the constructive greed that characterizes the 'rise' phase is Henry Ford paying his workers what were, for the time, unheard of high wages for an unheard of short workday. As witnessed by his actions when his workers later tried to form unions, he was not concerned with their welfare, but he did this so that they could afford to buy the cars his company made. Another example is Thomas Watson, Sr pioneering job security and fringe benefits for the workers of IBM. His motivation was that he wanted to keep them from organizing into unions. In this he was successful, but he did manage to build a strong loyalty among IBM workers.

The feeling that people have during this phase, of having a genuine stake in society's health and survival, is the substance of patriotism. The externals that accompany it are sincerely heartfelt. Even at the top of the wealth spectrum there is a sense of obligation to those who made that wealth possible: the workers whose labor creates that wealth, and the community in which one operates one's business.

An example of the destructive greed that causes the 'fall' phase is the wave of mergers and acquisitions that has been going on for some time. While fortunes are made no new jobs are created, and in fact, many are permanently lost. Accompanying this has been an abandonment of any commitment to workers and community; those are considered merely the means to augmenting those fortunes.

Of course, under these sorts of circumstances, the substance of patriotism evaporates. With no small amount of irony, there is an insistence on slavish adherence to those externals of patriotism that borders on idolatry. Coupled with that, there is also a naive call for a return to 'the virtues of our forefathers that made this country great'.

In the same vein, the name of some deity or other is invoked as somehow giving special protection to that country, as though this makes them exempt from the forces causing the decline. My view of this is that, after the time of the big bang, the only things that God has created are individual human souls, which are all equal before Him. Nations and other political subdivisions are strictly human creations and God is indifferent to their welfare or even their survival.

Another sign of the decay of a civilization is the way people's rights are dealt with. In the growth phase of a society, rights are recognized as being accompanied by responsibilities. There is also a realization of the fact that some rights may conflict with others, e.g. the right of a free press to report, as opposed to an accused person's right to a fair trial free from prejudicial pre-trial publicity. In this case, these disparate rights must be balanced one against the other, and an adjudication made for the public good. During the decline phase these things are negated in two ways. First, there is an increase in abuse of those rights. Worse yet, there is a growth of toleration of those abuses. Next, a number of special-interest groups start claiming that their group's rights are absolute and that should a conflict occur, all other rights must yield.

Fifteen centuries ago, St Augustine pointed out that it was vices that made a nation prosperous and powerful and that those same vices eventually would tear the nation down. I tend to share his pessimism about halting or reversing the process, but for very different reasons. Greed and pride are part of human nature, as is the rationalization of mistaking vices for virtues when the vices pay off. Lest I end on too pessimistic a note, another part of human nature is the ability to rise above that nature. However, it is likely the part that is least used.

Politics and religion

To what extent should they interrelate or interact? In the larger context mentioned in the chapter on religious topics, each person's metaphysical and ethical systems, whether they be religious, non-religious or even anti-religious, cannot help but form that person's outlook on political, social, and economic measures. For this reason, it is not fair to say either that 'religious values should rule our country,' or that 'religion should be kept out of politics, business, etc.'

Those who say such things in the hope that a particular viewpoint will be advanced should be cautioned. Examples abound of how liberal, moderate and conservative views all come from the religious and the non-religious alike.

It is my very strong belief that these philosophical issues have to be discussed and dealt with, if any rationality is to be introduced into a discussion of the role religion should play in any dialogue, ranging from our national political debates to a discussion that takes place in a relationship between two people (either budding or developed). With anything less, all will degenerate into cries of 'You're one!' and 'You're another!'

The previous discussion couched the topic in general terms, and I avoided my own views. Given what I said, this would be a good place to discuss them. As might be surmised, my beliefs on social and economic questions are derived from my religious beliefs. I have not mentioned political views, but these appear to spring from one's outlook on social and economic issues. This will likely raise no small amount of controversy, but it must be remembered that I am not trying to convince anyone of anything, but want to show how I form my opinions.

The basis for a religious requirement for a social conscience can be found in the place in the Gospels where Jesus Himself describes what the last judgement will be like, and in particular, what the criterion will be for separating the saved from the damned.[38] There is a great deal of use of metaphorical language, but it can be summarized.

Missing are things like failure to keep the Sabbath, blasphemy, thievery, adultery, or even murder. What is included can be summed up by: 'What was your attitude toward the most insignificant and down-trodden people in the world?' Put into modern American English: 'The homeless person, the teenage hooker, the person entangled by drugs or alcohol, the ex-con trying to go straight (often in vain), the abandoned unmarried mother, the mentally ill person shunned by others; I was all of them. When you gave them the cold shoulder, you gave me the cold shoulder.'

Conservatives have long rejected social programs because 'they would interfere with the marketplace'. Should social programs be avoided for that reason alone? That would be a short way of saying that they should be avoided because the wealthy would be taxed to pay for such programs, that profits might decline a bit, or that wealth and privilege might be threatened by them.

Liberals do not get off scot-free from this either. When *The Bell Curve* was published, it was denounced as racist.[39] (Its thesis was that the 15 per cent point advantage on standardized tests that white school children had over black students was the result of a race-based genetic inferiority on the part of black people.) This is basically a scientific hypothesis. It is undeniably racist, but suppose it happens to be correct? Are not those who denounce it on non-scientific grounds in the same company as those who for ideological reasons denounced Galileo, Darwin and Freud?

An excellent scientifically-based counterexample to the thesis of that book is Northern Ireland, where the same 15 point edge exists for Protestant over Catholic school children. They are all of the same race, but social and economic inequities exist there that are similar to those between white and black people in this country.

Why didn't those who were troubled by that book's thesis look to scientific experts to rebut it, instead of attacking it with an epithet that was well-deserved but unscientific? It is interesting to note that many of those who at the outset shouted 'racism' the loudest are the first to extoll 'free inquiry' and to denounce 'book burning' when it comes to ideas with which they agree.

I happen to believe that when it comes to a social conscience, a religious belief as I have previously defined it, is very desirable. I should like to give what is to me a prime example of someone whose social conscience was defined by his religion. I should then like to examine what I have seen happen all too often when a social conscience comes from purely secular motives.

The person in question is my favorite saint: Thomas More. Like me, all that he did and believed was governed by intellectual determinants. He was also a compromiser rather than a confronter. As Lord Chancellor to Henry VIII, he contacted the scholars of Europe to determine if there were arguments in favor of getting Henry the annulment he wanted from his marriage to Catherine of Aragon.[40] Yet when it came to the point at which compromise was no longer possible, i.e. when the king made himself head of the Church in England and demanded that all of his subjects recognize him as such, More accepted death rather than back down, although he tried everything humanly possible to avoid it. He did not whine about his fate as so many modern 'rebels' do about much lesser punishments, but even managed a bit of gallows humor at his execution. He asked somebody to help him climb up the steps of the scaffold, assuring him that he would have no problem getting down by himself.

More had a social conscience that was remarkable for any era, let alone the 16th century in which he lived. This can be seen in *Utopia*, his chief work. He believed that property owners should not have absolute control of how their property was used, decrying the fact that much of the land that belonged to the nobles was not being used, while landless farmers had nowhere to work. It might be noted here that the monasteries allowed these farmers to work land that they owned but did not need. It was for this reason that three centuries later, for closing those monasteries, Henry was vigorously condemned by none other than Karl Marx.

Thomas More also pointed out that there were root causes of crime other than the perversity of the criminals. In *Utopia*, he commented that the kingdom made thieves and beggars out of people and then punished them for being those things. He also deplored the gap that existed between the wealthy and the poor in his day. Realizing that there would always be differences in people with respect to talent, intelligence, and industriousness, he accepted that there would also be differences in wealth. But in the ideal society he envisioned in *Utopia*, nobody would be either too rich or too poor.

What of a social conscience that has no religious basis? (Remember the definition of 'religious' that was given before?) I must at this point enter a disclaimer. None of this should in any way be taken to mean that a social conscience with a secular basis is necessarily flawed. God knows, in these times (or for that matter, any other), the disadvantaged and downtrodden need all the allies they can get! However, I must direct attention to what is a key notion: 'durability'.

Going back to my definition of a religious belief, there does exist two questions that arise if a social conscience does not come from origins external to one's own intuitive inclinations.

The first is: in the absence of a moral imperative, what will make a person persevere should that person's interest wane? At the outset of the 'war on poverty' in the 1960s, many idealistic college students spent their vacation time, semester breaks, and even weekends, in the inner cities in order to help the children there. The special gifts that they brought were a cultural and intellectual awareness that demonstrated to those children that a better life did exist beyond that of the ghetto. This is beyond question something requiring a long-term commitment. Yet after very few years, they left to go back to the more traditional football-and-fraternity college lifestyle. It is interesting to note that Franciscan and Dominican nuns arrived at the same time. Unlike the college students, they are still there. The evidence seems to suggest that those college students who came and then left, came because of a 'feel-good' type of motivation and got bored when the novelty wore off. This would almost appear to be a vindication of Ayn Rand's cynical dictum that altruism is merely another form of selfishness.

The second question is: what will make a person persevere should his or her altruism seem to bear little or no fruit? Suppose programs to achieve a social goal do not pan out; will one keep going back to the drawing board and try to formulate programs that perhaps, will work? Suppose one comes to the realization that the social problem has no permanent solution; will one summon the necessary resolve to do what must be done indefinitely? It is easy to see how, lacking a motivation that comes from outside oneself, disillusionment and even cynicism can set in. Many times I have heard, 'I put myself out and they don't even appreciate it,' or, 'what good did it all do? They're as bad off as they ever were and probably always will be, so why should I bother?'

There is a group called the neo-conservatives. They share the belief of other conservatives that any social problems must look to the free marketplace for their solution. If some people's problems remain unsolved or even exacerbated by the marketplace, why that's too bad, but that's the way life is. Their big difference is that they were once liberals who championed social and economic justice. I know of none of them who were not secular in their liberalism.

The power, and limits, of government

During the 1960s, much legislation was enacted on civil rights and anti-poverty issues. These laws were designed to correct age-old injustices that had plagued the nation since the foundation of the republic. It was almost believed, at the time, that a new age of Pericles had arrived.

The previous period in which this sort of thing had been done was the 1930s, known as the New Deal era. During that time, the prime beneficiaries were working class people, and the government's actions were paralleled by the growth of strong labor unions. Indeed, much of that legislation was designed to aid and encourage that growth. In the 1960s, the prime beneficiaries were minorities and women. During both periods, the government was seen as an instrument for righting those social wrongs. By many, it was seen as *the* instrument.

There was, though, a major difference between those decades. The efforts of the 1930s seemed to yield universal benefits. The working class had been moved into the middle class. With the 1960s, large numbers of the intended beneficiaries seemed not to benefit. The social planners, appearing not to be willing to accept anything less than total success, looked for a reason, and found one: low self-esteem among many members of those groups.

My admittedly limited insight into human behavior finds it difficult to explain why this should be so but I do observe that, indeed, it does exist. (I can only think of one person who had no problem at all with self-esteem. That was Lucifer. He believed that he should be the equal of God, and self-esteem does not get any better than that.) Nevertheless, I have to ask: what can society, or government as the force behind the will of society, do about that? I have already said that the injustices that those laws were designed to correct were real and egregious. The laws not only opened doors that were previously closed to women and minorities, but also prescribed civil and criminal penalties against those who would close those doors again or stand in the way of anyone trying to walk through them.

What of those who, for one reason or another, do not walk through those now opened doors? Liberals appear to believe that the Government should do everything to correct social injustices, even to making sure that everyone benefits from correcting them. On the other hand, conservatives seem to believe that the Government should do nothing.

I think that they are both wrong. The Government should definitely open doors and keep them open. However, as to an individual wanting to walk through the open door, the Government is really quite powerless. For this, a person must look inside him or herself, with, one might hope, the assistance of their family and friends.

Any attempt to have society perform this very individual function all too often leads to two things: the creation of bureaucracies and industries that all too often give the appearance of having a personal stake in the problems not being solved, and the enactment of programs that are doomed to failure and that have the unfortunate side-effect of alienating public support for social legislation.

Social classes

This could also include economic classes, but the impetus for greater economic status is invariably linked to a drive to 'better' oneself socially, so that could be said to be a redundancy.

Americans claim to live by the dictum of Thomas Jefferson, in the Declaration of Independence, that all are created equal, by what he called 'The laws of nature and nature's God.' In what sense can this be taken? It would have to be that they are equal in their essences, or their souls. (This was not a novel idea. In the 12th century, the abbess, composer, and philosopher Hildegard von Bingen wrote that, in God's view, all souls are equal.) In creating social classes, humans are making people unequal in their existence. Do Americans really live by Jefferson's ideas? H.L. Mencken[41] demurred on this, stating that what Americans really desired was acceptance by those whom, for all their talk of equality, they recognize and accept as their betters.

I see the ethics of this as quite simple. The desire for appearing 'better' than others in the eyes of those others amounts to pride, the worst of the seven deadly sins. In order to achieve this, since one's status is manifest by the amount and opulence of one's possessions, one must accumulate as much of those as possible. This brings us to the second worst deadly sin: greed.

With one exception, the movies on religious topics that have come from Hollywood could be described by two adjectives: banal and superficial. The solitary exception was '*Oh, God,*' and it was unique in two respects. First, to be His prophet or messenger, God, played by George Burns, did not choose anyone from the secular or religious establishment, but instead picked a supermarket produce manager, played by John Denver. (This is quite consistent with the prophets chosen in the Hebrew scriptures.) Second, the message God wanted to reveal was one that went to the core of the way people live in an affluent society: that He had given humanity all that they could possibly need to live happy lives, i.e. full, rewarding, and productive.

If this is the case, then why is there so much privation in the world? Because there are some who insist on hogging more than their fair share. They do this to assert a social superiority over others, which is their version of happiness.

I was thinking about this in the wake of the school shootings that have plagued this country. The shooters, no matter what their social and economic status in the community, were at the bottom of the social ladder at school and were bullied for it. (Bullying has been decried, but when star athletes are allowed, without real fear of reprisal, to vandalize property and even rape girls, I am not too optimistic that anything meaningful will be done to curb school bullying.) When Columbine High School in Colorado, the site of the worst massacre, reopened, reporters, interviewing the students, found out that the pre-shooting pecking order of cliques was still alive and well. The surviving students had learned nothing.

In the aftermath of each incident, there was much preaching and punditry about how parents needed to teach values to their children. What do these high school students see at home? Their parents are contemptuous of those lower on the social and economic scales and envious of those higher up. It would appear that these young people have read their parents' values quite accurately, and liked them so much that they have decided to adopt them.

The upshot of all of this is that people tend to allow themselves to be defined by their social status and that this is defined by the pedigree of their ancestry or by the amount and opulence of their material possessions, and often both. A dissenting viewpoint comes from interesting sources. At the second Vatican council, there was a decree promulgated that Christians have a lot to learn from non-Christian religions. In particular, Buddhism was singled out because of its metaphysical teaching about the insufficiency of the material world.

This method of defining people in that manner has another defect. It denies the uniqueness of each person by allowing him or her to be defined by those who manage to promote themselves into the position of social arbiters, who thus are in a position to do so by tracing a pedigree and by measuring that amount and opulence of possessions. Given this, does there exist a method by which each person can be defined that respects his or her uniqueness? I believe that there is, and it consists of three things: what one knows, what one likes, and what one believes. These three things have one further advantage: they are the only things that I know of that one can give away to someone else and still keep for oneself.

Conclusions

A 'cure' for autism?

What is meant by a 'cure' for any condition? This question has to be addressed because so much of the effort in autism advocacy seems to be geared toward finding a cure. One definition that would appear to cover all conditions is: a permanent correction of the condition in question. In the case of autism, the implication is that the autistic person would, by some method, become non-autistic, or NT. Is this even feasible? We are now talking about rewiring a part of one of the temporal lobes in the brain that was either unwired or not properly wired. Any hopes of being able to do this involve biological research whose practical benefits are not seen as being available in the lifetimes of autistic people, adults or children, now alive.

For the foreseeable future parents, other relatives, and friends of autistic persons need to accept the fact that 'What you see is what you get.' Too many refuse to accept this, and cling to a false hope (false because it is based on a fiction) that inside an autistic person is a 'normal' person that only needs to be brought out. This harks back to the bad old days when autism was called 'childhood schizophrenia', and it was believed that it resulted from an emotional shock. I had hoped that this kind of attitude was behind us but it seems to be ubiquitous in the entertainment media. In an episode of a TV show called *Judging Amy*, there was a court battle the contention of which was to determine if a child was autistic, schizophrenic, or a victim of diabolical possession. (Yes, these were actually mentioned in the same breath; no comment is necessary.) I also saw a movie called *House of Cards*. The portrayal of an autistic girl was quite accurate, from being personally self-sufficient (unfortunately characterized later as withdrawal) to lack of any fear when she walked along the edge of a roof. This was totally ruined when in the denouement it was 'revealed' that her autism was triggered by witnessing her father's accidental death. She was 'cured', i.e. made normal by having to re-live that incident. (Freud lives!) I realize that stories such as that may be more profitable in the Nielsen ratings and at the box office, but they do a great disservice in creating false hopes by promoting false 'information'. I have my own way of appraising such 'entertainments' as these; they get my Bruno Bettelheim award.

Given that (for a while, anyhow) such a 'cure' is wishful thinking, what is to be done, especially for a child? I have mentioned before that, with autism, there are secondary traits that often accompany it. (Among these are ADD, speech difficulties, tic disorders, and so on.) These should be given timely corrective treatment as they would in any non-autistic child. As to the autism itself, efforts should be concentrated on making the child as high-functioning as possible. Patience should prevail while the child learns social skills in the only way he or she is able. Most of all, the child should, as early as practicable (practicable for the child not the parent), be made aware of who and what he or she is. From my own experience this gives new meaning to the old bromide: knowledge is power.

Given the breakneck pace of the advances in medical knowledge, it is not inconceivable that in this century a method will be devised of rewiring some or all sections of the human brain. This would definitely be a cure, as defined above. This may come as a shock to many but it might turn out to be a mixed blessing. This is a conclusion to which I have come after much soul-searching of my own and also from reactions that I have gotten from any number of Asperger and high-functioning people. To put this in context, since my discovery, I have often thought of myself as not unlike the character of Mr Spock in the TV series *Star Trek*. I have only seen, by comparison with devotees, a small number of episodes of that show. Many of those devotees have told me that, many times in that series, Mr Spock had spoken with some despair to Captain Kirk about the illogical behavior of humans, in that it visits all sorts of misery on themselves and others, many of whom they claim to like or even love. This is something that, in real life, has not escaped the notice of me and my fellow Vulcans. I remember how, after reading in the newspaper about a number of examples of this, I asked Alix almost rhetorically, 'Did you ever get the feeling that, as toddlers, we were abandoned on a planet populated by a bunch of lunatics?' She grinned and answered, 'You noticed.'

Both in my autobiography and in lectures that I have given, I have used the same analogy to describe the feeling I get when I am suddenly involved in people's out-of-control emotional situations: like a soldier who finds himself in the middle of a minefield. During one such lecture, I talked about what a cure would involve and wondered aloud if I would want such a thing. One woman in the audience said softly, 'You want to stay out of that minefield.'

While my temporal lobe (the source of the intuitive emotions) may be damaged, I still have my cerebral cortex intact (the source of reason and other 'executive' functions). Should a cure be found, what amount of certainty would I have that my cerebral cortex would rule, or at least guide, my newly-restored temporal lobe? From my observations of NT thinking and behavior I am not too optimistic. (This is sad, because I have often expressed the opinion that a person in possession of emotions, who had those emotions under the guidance of reason, could experience joys of living that I cannot even imagine.) Without such assurances, I believe that I would pass on that, as might many others. Nevertheless, should a repair become available, it should be a choice option, but should not be made mandatory.

Problems encountered in the world

How I would like to relate to the world, and vice versa

I have taken quite a few pages to explain many of my peculiarities to the non-autistic. And there is no need to paper over the fact that, in the eyes of the NT, they are peculiarities.

Some peculiarities can be considered harmless oddities in that, at worst, they might cause many to be uneasy in my presence. Unless the other person takes offense at anyone being different from him or herself, a mutual attitude of live-and-let-live is able to diffuse the situation.

Other peculiarities bring into question many of the values by which these NT people judge the world, themselves, and each other. (This is especially true if I do such things as fail to be impressed by their ostentatious displays of wealth or status.) The ideas that are represented by these oddities could be seen as threats by those people and, because of that, they might come to dislike me, perhaps even strongly.

What of that? There is a great deal of mythology (I don't know what else to call it) that this can be remedied by 'love' or 'acceptance'. Perhaps this might be asking too much of people. In my childhood, I read this short poem by Thomas Brown, an English satirist of the late 17th century:

> I do not love thee, Doctor Fell,
>
> The reason why I cannot tell;
>
> But this alone I know full well,
>
> I do not love thee, Doctor Fell.

Those that are honest (at least with themselves) will admit that there are, among those they know, any number of Doctor Fells. To this might be added those for whom we 'know the reason why'. These are people who, for one reason or another, 'rub our fur the wrong way'.

Any attempts to try to cultivate friendships among people who view each other that way will very likely exacerbate the mutual dislike. Is there a way of keeping the peace in cases like that? There is, but it goes against the aforementioned mythology. I once heard a starry-eyed young woman say, 'If there were only some way to get people to love each other.' The observation immediately occurred to me that humankind has been working on that approach for all of recorded history, with varying degrees of failure. I for one would be more than satisfied if there were a way to get people to simply be civil to each other. In other words, if there is someone for whom I am one of his or her Doctor Fells, I would say, 'OK. Look the other way and leave me alone.' The only thing I would like to ask is that if someone were to dislike me, it would be because of what I am actually all about, and not because of some misconception of me.

I find that I can peacefully coexist with any of the other six billion human souls on this planet, as long as they do not bother me or, at least, there is not the perception of being bothered. Even if a person cannot do this, I manage to tune out him or her. This may be because I have a thick skin, no chinks in my armor, or whatever it might be called. (NT people, on the other hand seem, in my view, to be overly afraid that others might find those chinks and exploit them.)

Yet there are conditions under which I would be bothered. This is when the person who dislikes me is in a position to do me some serious harm. A long time ago, I worked in a group with someone who viewed me that way for reasons I still consider trivial and intrusive. Being a serious music lover, I had a stereo sound system that while not prohibitively expensive, was the best that I could afford, and produced superb sound. Also, since my purpose in owning a car is to get me and mine from here to there reliably, safely, and economically, the car that I drove was the old VW Beetle. He once observed to a group of us: 'Ed spends a lot on his stereo and a little for his car. It should be the other way around.' At another time, he offered the opinion that my musical preferences, i.e. Wagner, Mahler, *et al.* and my indifference to Broadway musicals, cast doubts on my patriotism. In my own mind, I dismissed him as an incorrigible upscale yahoo, and had as little to do with him as possible. He wasn't worth arguing with, let alone coming to blows. Yet had he been promoted to a position in which he could have put in jeopardy the security clearance that I needed for my job, he and I would have had some interesting conversations.

At the beginning of this section, I commented that a great deal of the material in this book was written to explain my peculiarities. There is a very important practical reason why NT people should be made aware of why we are the way we are.

There are in the USA two laws that were designed to help people with disabilities. There is the ADA (Americans with Disabilities Act) and IDEA (Individuals with Disabilities Education Act). The former looks to the interests of the disabled in, among other things, the workplace; the latter does the same regarding the classroom. (It is much more complex than this, but this will suffice for our purposes.)

All too often, I read on the lists the complaints of parents about school officials, and others who 'just don't get it'. This is understandable because of the widespread ignorance of the precise nature of autism. Even with the legislation I mentioned, unless this ignorance can be remedied, it does little good. Congress can pass a bill (on any topic), the President can sign it into law, and the Supreme Court can uphold its constitutionality. Yet its effects on the public will not be felt until it has won the hearts and minds of the cop on the beat and the lowest level bureaucrat. Failure of proper implementation cannot always be ascribed to ill-will on the part of these people.

ADA and IDEA notwithstanding, an autistic person will not get a fair shake from either an employer or an educator who, with the best will in the world, is ignorant of the nature of autism. The job of providing the requisite information and insight is essential, but it is not something that will happen overnight.

Getting back to my being able to explain my peculiarities raises the question: what if I were among the non-verbal, and could not have explained those eccentricities? I would then be like the old lady in the story told in the first chapter. I would have been unable to explain the true situation to the boy scout and I would have missed my bus.

Social skills and sociability

The social skills of NT people are the result of two faculties that they possess. One is that of the intuitive emotions, which enables them to form bonds that appear to need no justification. The other is the ability to send and understand non-verbal 'signals'. The autistic are without either of these. What can they do to compensate? This is of no small importance since these skills are indispensable if they are to be able to function in society.

Disabilities such as blindness, lameness, and similar visible impairments can be easily recognized. Those who are disposed to be understanding and empathetic can easily make the required attitude adjustments to give them some slack. (Of course, those who are not will simply give them varying degrees of difficulty, no matter what disability is at issue.) Autism, because it is not so discernable, is another matter, especially if it involves Asperger people or those who are high-functioning. Even people of goodwill are less than sympathetic, mostly due to the vast amount of ignorance afoot.

To this must be added the mind blindness that affects all autistic people to one degree or another. Because of this, it can be difficult if not impossible to even guess the sincerity or intentions of another. Is someone actually agreeing with what has been said, or is that someone simply trying to avoid an argument? Is someone expressing his or her true feelings, or is he or she kidding around (to use an expression, 'pulling one's chain')? Is someone genuinely interested in what one has to say, or is that person concealing his or her boredom out of 'politeness'? When an autistic person offers to do something and the other person says, 'Sure', does the other person really want that to be done or is again simply being 'polite'? Imagine the difficulty the autistic person has in these instances in making social decisions. Opportunities for social gaffes are endless. The NT person, because of intuitive emotions and the 'ability to read signals' has no such difficulties (unless he or she is in denial).

How can the autistic compensate for this? One simple way is to simply guess (mentally 'toss a coin'). The problem here goes to a corollary of mine to Murphy's Law (if something can go wrong, it will).

This reads: if your chances of being right are 50–50, then nine times out of ten you'll be wrong. Something more dependable is required. To use a computer jargon analogy: for the NT, social skills are hard-wired; the autistic have to develop software. How can this be done?

As Dr Lorna Wing pointed out, the only way that these can be developed is that they be learned via the intellect. This, like any learning, is a gradual process, so that a child or young adolescent cannot be generally faulted for committing acts of *gaucherie* on purpose. A parent, friend, or relative must, like any teacher, be patient in the process of correcting, realizing that they cannot appeal to any inborn predispositions. It should go without saying that remarks like, 'you stupid oaf' are counterproductive for an autistic child, whereas, ironically, they might work for an NT child, who would change his or her behavior to avoid such embarrassments in the future.

What would such 'software' consist of? One type would be a list of 'thou-shalt-nots' and 'thou-musts', garnered gradually through experience. The other is a set of warning signs, obtained in the same way. These signs would be of two types. One is of the form, 'Falling rocks ahead; proceed with caution.' In this case, one must weigh the value of the destination to be reached against the perils that are likely to be encountered. The other is of the form, 'Bridge out ahead; do not proceed.' A person in touch with reality and not into denial will simply turn around, because proceeding would result only in having to wastefully retrace one's steps. (Someone who is totally into denial and not believing the sign will proceed at full speed, with results that are totally predictable.)

An autistic person will have to build up this 'software' through intellectual appreciation of lessons learned. Sometimes, with experience, these might have to be refined. An example is that a warning sign of the 'falling rocks' category will have to be upgraded to one of 'bridge out'. This is something that takes time because it is not innate.

I might point out that while they do enable people to live with others in an atmosphere of minimal conflict, social skills are not always good things in themselves. For one thing, successful deceivers, in order to be successful, need good social skills. In another (somewhat infamous) case, some time between his arrest and later execution, Timothy McVeigh who in April 1995 set off the bomb that killed 168 people (some young children) in a federal office building in Oklahoma City, spent time in the same federal prison in which Theodore Kaczynski, the Unabomber, was serving his life sentence. The two got to know each other and seemingly became friends. After McVeigh was sent away to another prison, someone asked Kaczynski what he thought of him. The answer was that he liked him very much and praised him for his 'excellent social skills'.

Problems at school

As I mentioned earlier, I graduated from high school when autism was first identified as a distinctive syndrome so there was no choice for me other than what is now called 'mainstreaming'. A number of the details of my education process were given in my autobiography, in the chapter titled *Learning*.[42]

I had many sociability problems in school. This pertains to a number of posts on the lists from parents of pre-pubescent children who say that their child is terribly unhappy about not 'fitting in'. I had to wonder about that, because one of the prime autistic traits is that of being a loner. It is certainly true about Alix and me. I then happened to remember myself at that age and realized that I was that way also. Why would that be? The reason was because of many things such as ethnicity, religion (I had none), and temperament: I was a natural outsider. Among children this is a short step to being an outcast and led to the inevitable bullying. I realize now that then as now I would have preferred just to be left alone by those who would dislike me for any reason. However, at that young age my intellectual appreciation of social situations had not developed to the point that I would recognize that as an option. To me at that age the only viable options were 'belonging' or being bullied. No prizes are offered for guessing which I would have chosen if I could. Because of this, I wanted inclusion as much as the children of those parents who posted about that, but for the autistic that does not come easy. I managed to survive until such time as I could build what Jasmine Lee O'Neill calls my 'portable sanctuary'.[43] This happened in my high school, which was not your usual high school. As a way of explanation, the High School of Music and Art was one of a group of schools unique to New York City, which were founded when Fiorello LaGuardia was mayor. They offer the full academic program, together with a concentration in some specialty. Two others are the Bronx High School of Science and Brooklyn Technical High School. At M and A, as we called it, there was a student body, each member of which marched to his or her own unique drummer. Even in a setting like that, I did not quite fit in, but I was tolerated and even liked by many, perhaps because of my idiosyncrasies. I came to realize that there did exist that option which, in the lower grades, I would have dearly loved.

I have mentioned the difficulty I had in reading, due to my ADD. I have since come to realize how I manage to compensate for that. To put it in context, if a student buys a used textbook, the buyer can expect to find important passages highlighted in yellow (or some other prominent but nondescript color). I find that I am able to skim over the text and my attention is drawn, how I do not know, to the pertinent passages (the ones that would have been highlighted). For example, I am reading an article about someone in whose ideas I have an interest. The writer gives all kinds of irrelevant details, such as the flower beds outside his front door, the design and colors of the tie he is wearing, and so forth. I am able to skip over such trivia (which seems to be essential to many readers) and go straight to the part in which he talks about the issues at hand. Also, I sometimes 'read' a newspaper or magazine by skimming over the pages. Quite often, my attention will be drawn to a key word in an article I would want to read as if it were highlighted. A terrific example of this is the article by Oliver Sacks, from which I learned about my autism. My gaze was drawn to that first subtitle sentence: 'Can an artist make art without feeling it?'

This is not an exclusively autistic trait. My daughter, totally NT, as part of the work she does has to go over government documents. They seem to be designed to obfuscate rather than enlighten. She skips over the bureaucratese and goes directly to the information that she needs to make her decisions. Obviously, she inherited this faculty from me, but I developed it as compensation for my ADD.

Many have told me that they are amazed at my long-term memory, especially for things that go back years, even decades. The way it appears to work is that when something happens, whatever is done and said is put into something like a peripheral storage device. When I am thinking about something, either by myself or in a conversation, some key words are seemingly put into a processor, which then searches that peripheral storage and retrieves the 'files' that pertain to those thoughts in great detail. People tend to be amazed at how I remember something they had told me a long time ago and I have been accused of holding those things in my mind to spring on them at a later time. I do not do that; it is completely involuntary, but trying to explain that usually makes matters worse. It could be said that I have a search engine for a memory.

Problems in the workplace

The pivotal incident in my autobiography was the nervous breakdown that I suffered in June 1978.[44] Since the purpose of mentioning that was to show how circumstances led to the discovery of my autism, I did not dwell on the details of what caused that breakdown. Since those details are quite relevant to the problems faced by the autistic in the course of their employment, they will be discussed here.

There are a couple of items dealt with in that book that I should like to briefly revisit. One is that I was considered unpredictable by my managers. This could be ascribed to the fact that my motivations and values were so different from those of my co-workers. The other is that I worked best on tasks in which I worked by myself. (I called this being a 'one man band'.) Even when working on a project with others, I did best when I could carve out a section of that project all for myself. There were other problems as well.

I am neither ambitious nor competitive. This makes me not a 'self-promoter', from which it follows that I am not a corporate 'pyramid climber'. Many other autistic people are like that. (I suspect that I could say 'most' instead of 'many', but I haven't taken a poll.) This is certainly an impediment to climbing the corporate ladder. While this might not be an issue of major concern to an autistic employee, as long as he or she does not see him or herself as being exploited, it can be a cause of friction between the employee and an NT spouse, especially if the spouse is a 'social climber'. This is because, for the NT spouse, one's position in the corporate hierarchy consti- tutes no small part of his or her sense of self-worth.

Many managers that I have come across (and a few that I have worked for), in motivating their employees, see themselves as being like football coaches, and the projects tasked to their departments as 'touchdowns' to be scored. Departmental meetings have all of the trappings of 'locker room pep talks'. Being self-motivated, as are many autistic people with whom I have communicated, I do not respond to this approach, and spend the time at such meetings in filtering out the essential information needed to do my job. To such a manager, this comes across as apathy when indeed it is not. I could never convince such a manager that I was not apathetic so I do not have any concrete suggestions as to how to deal with this specific problem.

A greater problem for an autistic employee is what is called 'work- place politics'. This could be defined as a situation where, instead of working together toward the common goals, individuals, especially managers, work at cross-purposes to each other. They hope to advance themselves by denigrating the efforts of those others. There will be a great deal of manipulation in this sort of environment. Also, if not outright dishonesty, there will be lack of candor and honesty. I know that I have no defense against this sort of thing. Furthermore, my mind blindness makes it quite difficult, if not impossible, to see what there might be beyond that lack of candor. It was a situation just like this that caused me to become bewildered to the point at which I suffered what I call 'a paralysis of the will' (this is often mistaken for depres- sion). It led to my nervous breakdown.

Lastly, to some it might be stretching the definition to include the Army as part of the 'workplace', but there are similarities in terms of optimum use of its personnel. I served the last two years of my tour of duty as a commissioned officer. The best commanding officer that I had was candid enough to tell me that he felt that I was miscast as an officer in the infantry or any other of the combat arms (artillery or armor), and that I would do better in one of the technical services (ordnance, chemical corps, and so on). In retrospect, I would have gone further than that. There is a personnel category called 'warrant officer'. They are considered officers and have the appropriate privileges, but they are there as experts in something and are never given command responsibilities. I believe that I could have been very comfortable in such a role. There is an Asperger man whom I consider an e-mail pen friend. Upon graduation from college he received a commission from the Reserve Officers Training Corps (ROTC) program. On active duty he became a helicopter pilot. These are normally warrant officers, but as a commissioned officer he was made a commander of a helicopter unit. By his own admission, he did not do as well as he would have liked. (For that matter, neither did I.) We agreed with one another that had we been warrant officers, we likely would have made a career out of the military.

In regard to the problems discussed here, perhaps a corporate effort to train managers in understanding the nature of autism might help, as it should in the case of any disability. Since the deficits of autism are not as readily discernible as those of other disabilities, this would be especially important.

The worst part of my autism

What was the worst part of my autism? The answer to that question is simple, direct, and easy: not knowing about it. Had I been not so high-functioning, I very likely would have been considered mentally retarded and in all likelihood would have been institutionalized. Very likely, it would have been for my entire life.

Being AS has its drawbacks also. When one is that high-functioning, then from those ignorant of the AS person's autism, NT things are expected, with the social penalties that are easily predicted. (When the autistic person is themself ignorant of their condition, there are no defenses at all.) He or she is expected to be sociable, to be a team player, to be a mixer, to pick up the signals of others – the list goes on.

This is also partially true of the HFA, especially when they are gifted in some way or other. Alix is talented and creative in designing and building web sites; they reflect her sense of humor. Seeing them, it might be assumed that she would be the life of the party. Yet because her speech does not quite reach the level of her writing, she tends to be reticent as far as social contacts are concerned. Trying to ask someone like that to go to social gatherings is like inviting a blind person to go to an art exhibition. The unease experienced by both should be understandable.

The pity is that even in social situations the autistic have a great deal going for them. For one thing, as Dr Lorna Wing wrote to me in her letter, '…they are capable of kindness and generosity sometimes well beyond that found in the "neurologically typical"'. In addition, Paul Shattock, in writing about Alix and me, said that because we are 'head people', '…you deduce the most appropriate way to act'. The problem is that because we appear to be aloof and standoffish, we are rarely if ever given credit for these things.

The only thing that rescues us from bewilderment is the knowledge of who and what we are. Had I known this for all of my life, things would have been vastly different. I would have made many other choices than the ones that I did. I could have tried to explain myself to the clueless. Ironically, now knowing my limitations, I have actually been more comfortable in social situations than I was before my self-discovery.

To describe the benefits of self-knowledge, words fail me, and that does not happen too often. I spent six decades of my life searching for the right size round hole for myself. Since then I have been digging my own square hole. The old platitude is absolutely right: you have to play the hand you were dealt. It helps greatly to know which cards you have and what the rules of the game are.

Self-image and self-acceptance

I have often seen posts on the lists from parents of autistic children complaining of the children's gullibility, and how this causes them to be taken advantage of by others. When I was young, I myself was often taken to task for this by members of my family who had no idea that I did not choose to be like that and could not choose to be otherwise. This could definitely be put at the door of my mind blindness. It is not unlike a visually blind person who, when asking for change for a ten dollar bill, is given only two one dollar bills and told that he or she is being given two fives. He or she has absolutely no equipment to know otherwise, and will not find out what has happened until one of two things takes place: an attempt is made to spend one of those fives, or a really good friend points out that he or she has been cheated.

There was an experience that I had at the age of 14 that foretold what I would go through in years to come. It was a year after the end of the Second World War. I would sometimes hang out with a small group of young teenagers. Close by was a group of men in their early twenties and their girlfriends. The men had just returned from the war. One of the men took a strong dislike to me. Why, to this day I do not know. He lost no opportunity to make nasty remarks to me, which was not too often since I avoided him whenever possible. Nevertheless, it was often enough.

Because I avoided him as much as I could, while I was uncomfortable, those remarks did not cause me any pain. (I have already mentioned my thick skin.) Since any anger that I may have experienced about this was purely situational, I did not harbor any grudges toward him. This may seem odd but during the periods between those barbs, I found myself seeing him in a rather sympathetic light. I confided this to one of the older couples (nobody else in that group showed me any animosity at all). Knowing how that man acted toward me, the woman smiled and said, 'That's sweet of you.' The man shook his head and said, 'I hope that there's a heaven for you to go to, because in this world everyone is going to crap all over you.'

During the decades that followed, not knowing about being autistic, I would often wonder what I could possibly do to quit being like that. I would go through alternating periods of trusting people too much and cynically trusting nobody.

Another characteristic of mine, possibly related to constantly feeling like an outsider, was that I treated both praise and undeserved criticism the same; I shrugged my shoulders at both. Yet when I was given praise, I was somewhat happy to get it, but not as ego enhancement in the way that NT people do. I realize that the reason is the same as I have read in correspondence that I have had with AS and HFA people. Because we live as outsiders, there is a nagging awareness of a precarious tenure on this planet. Recognition of our accomplishments are not the boosters of self-esteem that they are with the NT, but instead indicators that perhaps we will continue to be tolerated.

For these reasons and others, among the NT it is a given that the self-image of an autistic person has got to be rather low. This is because they see a penchant for solitude and other such things and apply NT standards to those. That assessment would be quite valid were the person not autistic. Now any self-appraisal would have to be, by its very nature, self-serving. So as evidence to the contrary, I would like to tell of a few incidents in which others sized me up on that.

When I was in the US Army before I became an officer, I served 17 months in the enlisted ranks. When I was stationed overseas, I made friends with another soldier who had graduated from a 'party college'. While I had spent my undergraduate college years immersed in my studies, mostly in the arts and humanities, he had, true to the nature of his school, spent it partying. (While he did do well enough in his classes to graduate, I would have to say that from his reports, he majored in fraternities, minored in sororities, and went to classes as an extra-curricular activity.) He always found my efforts to steer the conversation in the direction of topics such as literature and philosophy a source of amusement, and would regale me about the wild times that he had. During one lull in the conversation, I mused about how my approach to enjoying life was to get my pleasures from things that are substantial and enduring rather than superficial and transitory. His demeanor suddenly became quite serious and he said to me, 'Ed, you will never know how much I envy you your ability to do that.' I was a bit surprised by this because at the time it was obvious to me that he could have made a similar choice, and I wondered why he had chosen not to.

In the early 1970s, one of my co-workers dropped into my office for a chat. During the conversation he said, 'I have noticed, and so have others, that you seem to be a man who is very satisfied with the kind of person you are.' I was at a loss for words for an answer, because I could not see why I should be able to do that when others seemingly could not.

In the late 1970s, when I was talking to one of my colleagues about the cultural resources in the area, he said that while he did go to them occasionally, he marveled at the way that I actively sought them out. When I mentioned this to another co-worker, he said to me, 'Many people here have noticed in you a zest for living that it's very hard to duplicate.' If one were to apply to me the standard NT formulae for happiness, my dispassionate way of dealing directly with people would mark me as lonely and unable to 'relate'. Yet these incidents show that in my own self I have managed, in a way that is often evident to others, to live a good life with autism.

A Light-Hearted Epilogue

Paul Shattock, in his e-mail to me, wrote that '...the "head" as opposed to the "heart" people realize that life is a joke rather than a tragedy'. I should like to finish by giving examples of this.

When I first started posting with an autism list that was sponsored by St John's University in New York City, I was perusing the posts one day and was startled to see one with the subject line:

EVERYBODY PLEASE READ THIS! (Caps hers.)

The message simply read:

ANYBODY OUT THERE KNOW WHAT IT'S LIKE TO BE ADOLESCENT AND AUTISTIC? (Again, caps hers.)

Having fit that category, I replied to her privately. She turned out to be a teenage girl in England who had recently been diagnosed with autism, but who didn't quite understand what it was all about. We started an e-mail dialogue, which included me sending her my auto-biography (then in an embryonic stage). She would tell me of things such as being called a 'retard' by her school classmates, but she said that it didn't bother her. I told her that this was normal for autism. It continued like that until she started at a special college for the autistic.

In her last e-mail message to me, she ended by saying, 'I don't post to the lists quite as much as I used to. I usually reply directly – fed up with getting flamed by people misunderstanding what I say.' To this I replied, 'That's been a problem all my life. We just don't think the way the NT do.' She replied, 'Who would want to think the way they do? It's too illogical for me!'

Another example is something that was said not only in my book, but also in Jasmine Lee O'Neill's *Through The Eyes Of Aliens.*[45] (If you have not read it, I strongly urge you to do so.) Jasmine and I could be said to have been at opposite ends of the autistic spectrum – she did not speak (a faculty that, joyfully, she has since recovered) and many may likely wish that I would follow suit. (The only speech difficulty that Asperger people have is not knowing when to shut up.) Nevertheless, we both share the view that we are very capable, in our own unique way, of making happy lives for ourselves. The only thing that is needed is that nobody should try to change us into something that we are not.

I have already written on how autism can be self-compensating.[46] This was not lost on Father Neil when I was telling him about Alix's medical problems. Day in and day out, he deals with those who cannot seem to solve their problems, not because solutions are non-existent or unfeasible, but because of the emotional baggage that they carry around. He said to me, at the end of one of our gab fests, 'Ed, when I die and get to purgatory, my first request will be that God make me autistic so I can relax.'

APPENDIX A

Ed's Recipes

(Needless to say, they are not for the timid of palate.)

Spätzle

The only way I have been able to describe this item is as 'German pasta'. You might note that the recipe is somewhat bland. That was done on purpose. Many of the dishes served with it are quite heavily flavored. I did not want this to clash with any of them. It is designed solely to give the eater that nice, replete, and fulfilled feeling.

Ingredients
¾ cup milk
2 cups flour
2 eggs, beaten
½ teaspoon salt

Boil a large pot of water. Add one teaspoon of salt.

Using a spätzle maker, or a colander with ¼ inch holes, hooked on the edge of a pot over vigorously boiling water, push the dough through the holes into the water. Stir it often.

Boil the dough until it is done (10 minutes should do it), stirring it often, and testing it by texture after the spätzle rises to the top of the boiling water.

Drain it, toss it with butter or margarine (optional), and serve it.

Sauerbraten

This is a classic German beef dish. (The 'sauer' refers to the acid content of the vinegar used in the marinade.) The strong flavorings are a throwback to the days before refrigeration. Then, for obvious reasons, they were a necessity; now they can be a pleasure. This is, to my mind, the only way to make this item. The flavors permeate through and through. If one is making it commercially, this method is likely not to be cost-effective.

Ingredients

5 pounds lean beef
1 tablespoon salt
3 chopped onions
2 tablespoons mixed pickling spices
3 chopped carrots
3 stalks chopped celery
1 teaspoon dried thyme
1 quart apple cider vinegar
1 box gingersnaps
1 jar redcurrant jelly
36 ounces beer*

Place the beef in a large non-reactive container. Add the onions, carrots, celery, vinegar, beer, and salt (this is the marinade).

Place the pickling spices and thyme into a steel or plastic spice ball or (if you want it to be difficult) place them onto several layers of cheesecloth, forming a small bag, and tie it securely. Add it to the marinating beef. Refrigerate the beef in the marinade, covered, for one week. Turn the beef twice each day.

When you are ready to cook, remove and discard the spices.

Place the beef and marinade, including the vegetables, into a large non-reactive cooking vessel. Cook, at just below boiling, for 2–2½ hours. Turn the meat over after 1–1½ hours.

Remove the beef from the marinade and slice it. Blend the marinade as follows: fill the blender to the ¾ full mark with the marinade (including the vegetables). Add 6 ginger snaps and 2 tablespoons of redcurrant jelly. Blend it at medium speed until it is smooth. Repeat this to use all of the marinade.

Return the meat and gravy to an oven proof serving dish. Cool it in the refrigerator until it is cold then cover it with aluminum foil. To enhance the flavor, it may be stored overnight in the refrigerator.

Reheat prior to serving, in a 300 degree oven, until it is sufficiently warm. Then set the oven to the 'warm' setting until it is ready to be served.

Serve with spätzle or buttered noodles; mashed potatoes are also fine.

* Non-alcoholic beer may be used.

German Potato Salad

The main comment I should like to make about this recipe is that given the list of ingredients, there is nothing that would cause food poisoning, a major problem with other forms of potato salad, especially at things like picnics or any other gatherings. Of course, this can be pushed a bit. I would not recommend leaving it in the sunlight for a couple of days.

Ingredients

5 pounds potatoes
1 teaspoon salt
1 pound bacon
2 tablespoons sugar
1 medium onion, finely chopped*
apple cider vinegar

Boil the potatoes for ½ hour.

Cut the bacon into ½ inch-wide strips. Fry it until just before it becomes crisp. Drain the bacon, saving the liquid grease residue. Measure the amount of the liquid grease, and add an equal amount of cider vinegar. Set this aside in some container. It will separate, so don't worry about that.

Drain the potatoes. Peel them or not, as preference might dictate. Cut the potatoes into slices and place them in a large bowl. (I use the pot in which I boiled them. Why not?)

Sprinkle the salt, sugar, and chopped onions over the potatoes.

Reheat and mix the bacon grease and vinegar combination until the mixture is hot and well blended. Pour at once over the potatoes. Mix it all well.

Let it stand for the flavors to blend. Add the bacon pieces before serving. Mix it well.

* If you're not into masochism, the onions can be run through a micro-food processor instead of being chopped with a knife.

Filling for Schwarzwälderkirschschokoladetorte

This lengthy German word translates as 'Black Forest cherry chocolate cake'. (They have a way of combining many words into one.) Any good chocolate cake mix can be used but you can make your own from scratch; for me, it is not worth the bother. This is the only filling that I know of that uses whole cherries. I do not use whipped cream for the topping. (Or *schlag*, if you must be *echt*.) When the filling has been spread between the cake layers, there is always a fair amount of glop that is left in the saucepan. This can be spread over the top instead.

Ingredients
1 10 ounce can red tart pitted pie cherries in water
   (do not use canned pie filling!)
2 tablespoons corn starch

¼ cup sugar
¼ teaspoon almond extract

Open the can of pie cherries. Using a strainer to catch the cherries, pour the juice into a saucepan. Add the corn starch and stir it until it is completely dissolved. Add the sugar and stir it until it is completely dissolved. Add and stir in the almond extract.

Heat it, using the highest heat, while stirring constantly. It will become thick after a while, and little dark specks will appear. Shortly after, when it becomes totally dark and thick, remove it from the heat and stir in the cherries. Continue stirring it until the cherries are mixed in thoroughly. Do not add it to the cake until both the cake and filling have cooled.

If the cake is of the double-layer variety (made in two 9" circular cake pans), spread the filling in between the layers. Scrape any of the residue from the saucepan and spread it over the top of the cake.

If the cake is rectangular (made in a 13" x 9" cake pan), make two fillings and spread them over the top of the cake.

Spinach Cream Cheese Casserole

This is a good quickie thing to make. It's especially good if one needs, for the occasion, something out of the ordinary, but meat-free.

Ingredients
1 8-ounce pack cream cheese (softened)
1 8-ounce pack of stuffing mix
3 packs frozen spinach
1½ sticks butter

Allow the spinach to warm to room temperature.

Melt one stick of butter in a large saucepan. Add the stuffing and stir and toss it until the stuffing pieces are coated and lightly browned. Save this.

Separately, add ½ stick of butter and the softened cream cheese to the spinach in the pan. Heat it gently to melt the butter and cream cheese completely. Blend it well with the spinach.

Mix the spinach concoction together with the stuffing mix in a casserole or loaf pan.

Bake at 350 degrees for 30 minutes. Stir well before serving.

Banana Bread (A low-fat version)

This makes a good snack for diabetics or any other people on restricted diets. Warning: do not try to substitute for eggs or sugar. The taste will suffer and in terms of texture, the results are disastrous. It is best when the bananas that are used are in the proper state of 'rotten-ness'. Those bananas can be frozen and then thawed prior to using them in this recipe.

Ingredients
½ cup unsweetened applesauce
½ teaspoon salt
¾ cup sugar
½ teaspoon baking soda
2 eggs
2 medium sized bananas
1 ¾ cup all purpose flour
3 tablespoons milk (full fat, semi or skimmed)
1 tablespoon baking powder

Cut up the bananas.

Mix, in a large bowl, the milk, applesauce, and sugar. Add the eggs and beat it all well. Mix together, in a separate bowl, the flour, baking powder, salt, and baking soda. Add it to the liquid mixture and mix it until it is thoroughly mixed. Add the cut up bananas to the batter and blend it well. Preheat the oven to 350 degrees. Grease a loaf pan (9" x 5" x 3" or thereabouts) and pour the batter into it. Bake it for 60 minutes (or more, in 5 minute increments, if it is not yet done – I test it with a toothpick, which should come out dry). Remove it from the pan and cool it on a rack. If it is to be eaten the next day, wrap it up in a sealable plastic bag and store it overnight in the refrigerator.

It is best eaten at room temperature but if a loaf is to be cut into pieces, it should be firmed up in the refrigerator first.

This item freezes very well (something to think about if it must be made well in advance, or if there are any leftovers). In this case, let it thaw overnight in the refrigerator before eating.

Chicken Enchiladas

Courtesy of my oldest son, Christian, who got this recipe from a Mexican-American girlfriend when he was stationed at Camp Pendleton, while serving in the United States Marine Corps.

This is a recipe that is a bit cumbersome but worth the effort for a special occasion. I usually prepare the chicken the day before, and then keep it overnight in a sealed container in the refrigerator. I have never found the like in any Hispanic restaurant. It can also be made with low or no-fat ingredients.

Ingredients

1 can tomatoes (approx 1.5 lbs)
2 4-ounce. cans chopped green chillies
3–3½ teaspoons coriander
3–3½ teaspoons salt
2 cups dairy sour cream
1 8-ounce packet cream cheese
4 cups cooked chopped chicken
5–5¼ teaspoons salt
1 small finely chopped onion
1 cup shredded meltable cheese
16 6-inch flour tortillas

A good rule of thumb is that 1 lb of chicken, cooked and boned, makes one cup.

Take the cream cheese out of the refrigerator and allow it to soften.

In a chopper, finely chop the tomatoes (skip this step if using crushed tomatoes). Blend the coriander in with the tomatoes.

Mix together the chicken, cream cheese, onion, and 5–5¼ teaspoons of salt.

Dip the tortillas individually into the tomato mixture. Fill each tortilla with some chicken mix and roll it up. Place it, seam side down, in an ungreased baking dish (a lasagna pan will do). Add the sour cream, 3–3½ teaspoons salt, and chillies to the rest of the tomato mixture. Blend it well and spread it evenly over the rolled stuffed tortillas.

Cover it with aluminum foil. Preheat the oven to 400 degrees and bake it for 30 minutes. Remove the foil, add the shredded cheese, raise the heat to 500 degrees, and bake it for 10 more minutes.

Since two of these are plenty, this serves eight people. It goes great with rice (Spanish or plain).

Bulgarian Goulash

The only thing that I know is Bulgarian about this, is that my oldest son, Christian, got it from a mess sergeant who was born in Bulgaria, when he served in the United States Marine Corps. It is a spicy-and-sweet item, which is somewhat thick.

Ingredients
3 pounds lean meat
3 tablespoons curry powder
1 ⅓ sticks butter
¾ cup honey
4 tablespoons ginger
⅓ cup cornstarch
5 tablespoons paprika
salt and pepper to taste

Cut the meat into small pieces.

Put the butter and ginger into a pot. Heat it to the point at which the butter is boiling vigorously. Put the meat into the pot and brown it. Add the paprika and curry powder. Stir it. Add one cup of water and cover the pot, but not tightly. Simmer it at just under boiling for two hours. Stir it after one hour. The juice should boil down some. After the two hours, add the honey and mix it well.

Dissolve the cornstarch completely into a small amount of water. Add it to the pot and mix it well immediately. Bring it up to a boil. Stir it until the juice is at the desired thickness.

Serve it over rice, boiled potatoes, noodles, or spätzle.

Piroshki

This is a filled pastry. It is a bear to make, but really is worth the effort. It is not to be confused with *pirogi*, which is peasant fare. The ingredient list shows it to be aristocratic. One must be prepared to spend all day making something that will disappear in minutes. It is called an appetizer, but it is so hefty that it bears out one of my contentions: that appetizers have the same relationship to the appetite that birth control has to birth.

Pastry Ingredients

2 sticks butter
8 ounces cream cheese
¼ cup heavy cream
2½ cups flour
1 teaspoon salt

Filling Ingredients

3 tablespoons butter
2 finely chopped onions
1 pound lean ground beef
1–1¼ cups sour cream
¼ teaspoon tabasco
¼ cup cooked rice
1 teaspoon dried dill
½ teaspoon salt
½ teaspoon pepper
2 chopped hard-boiled eggs

To make the pastry dough: bring 2 sticks of butter and the cream cheese to room temperature then blend them in a mixer. Blend in the flour and salt. Wrap the resulting dough in waxed paper and chill it in the refrigerator for at least one hour before using it.

To make the filling: in a skillet, heat 3 tablespoons of butter and sauté the onions until they are golden brown. Add the ground beef and cook it until it is lightly browned. Remove it from heat and drain off any excess fat. Add the sour cream, tabasco, cooked rice, dill, salt, pepper, and hard-boiled eggs. Preheat the oven to 400 degrees.

Take one coffee spoon of pastry dough and flatten it out. Place one coffee spoon of filling on it. (This will have to be done for each of them.) To make piroshki, fold the dough over the filling. Place each of the piroshki onto a greased baking sheet. Bake them until they are golden (it should take about 15 to 20 minutes).

The piroshki should be eaten at room temperature and may be served with sour cream or eaten as is. They may also be frozen, but should be thawed in the refrigerator prior to being eaten.

Tvorozhniki (Russian cheese cakes)

This item must be made to order. The cakes have to be fried right then and there, before serving. However, the batter could be made beforehand and transported to the site. The kissel, which is then poured over it, has to be served when it is made. If it is allowed to stand, even while heated, it dries up into a substance that could be used for caulking.

Ingredients

1 pint ricotta cheese
½ cup flour
1 teaspoon baking powder
1 teaspoon grated lemon rind
1 teaspoon vanilla (real)
⅓ cup sugar
1 beaten egg

In a blender, mixer, or food processor, mix the ricotta cheese until it is smooth. Transfer it to a small bowl. Combine the cheese with the flour, baking powder, lemon rind, vanilla, sugar, and egg.

Chill it for at least an hour. With well-floured hands, form the chilled cheese mixture into flat round cakes, about 2 inches across and ½ inch thick. Sauté the cakes slowly in butter, over medium heat on both sides, until they are golden. Serve them hot with apricot kissel.

They may be reheated, but aren't as good.

Apricot Kissel

Ingredients
1 pound dried apricots
1 12 ounce can apricot nectar
1 ½ teaspoons grated lemon rind
½ cup sugar
1 cup water

Combine the apricots with the nectar and water in a 2 quart saucepan. Allow to stand for several hours or overnight.

Cook covered, over very low heat until it is tender (about 20 to 25 minutes). Let it cool slightly. Purée in a blender. Add the sugar and lemon rind. Blend well.

Pour it over the tvorozhniki.

German Cheesecake

There should be a Surgeon General's warning on this recipe. It is cholesterol city, and is guaranteed to plug up your aorta with the first bite. Any attempt to circumvent this by using no-fat ingredients will result in something totally unpalatable. It is designed not to have a topping, but I have included an option for having one.

Ingredients
4 8 ounce pack cream cheese
4 eggs
1 cup sugar
¼ cup heavy cream
½ tablespoon real vanilla extract (bourbon an acceptable substitute)

Bring the cream cheese and eggs to room temperature. Beat the cream cheese with strong beaters (or a paddle) until it gets to be smooth. Slowly add the sugar while beating until it is totally mixed. Remove the beaters from the bowl of the mixer. Scrape the beaters into the bowl and scrape bottom of the bowl.

Place a whisk (if paddles were used) onto the mixer. Otherwise, continue to use the beaters. Turn the beater onto the highest speed for three minutes. At the end of each minute, stop, and scrape the sides and bottom of the bowl.

At this point, preheat the oven to 450 degrees.

Add the eggs, one at a time. For each egg, beat the mixture at high speed until the egg is thoroughly mixed in. Between each egg, stop the mixer, and scrape the sides and bottom of the bowl.

Pour and beat in the cream and vanilla.

Grease the sides and bottom of a springform pan, 10" in diameter and 3" deep. (A 3" deep rectangular pan approximately 78 square inches in area can also be used.)

Pour the mixture into the pan. Leave any lumps in the bowl. It is important to place something under the springform pan, or else grease will drip onto the oven burner. Put it on the low rack of the oven for 15 minutes.

Turn the oven off. Remove and let it cool on a rack for ½ hour.

Put it back into the oven and bake it at 250 degrees for two hours.

Remove and cool it on a rack until it reaches room temperature.

Refrigerate it at least overnight, but three days is better. Cover it loosely with aluminum foil after one day. If it is baked in a springform pan, remove the sides for easier serving.

This can be frozen.

This is best made without a topping, because the two 'sweetnesses' will tend to compete with each other. If some topping is desired, then the recipe should be modified. The one cup of sugar should be omitted and the ¼ cup of heavy cream should be increased to ½ cup.

Chicken Paprikas
(Pronounced 'paprikash')

This is a variation on a traditional Hungarian dish. I have modified it slightly to make it easier to eat. There is no graceful way to eat chicken from the bone completely and this is too good to waste any. At the beginning of Bram Stoker's novel *Dracula*, this is the dish eaten in a restaurant by Jonathan Harker, the hero of the story, on his arrival in the small town in Hungary near Castle Dracula.

Ingredients
4 pounds chicken
2 large onions
3 tablespoons butter
2 tablespoons paprika
1 cup tomato sauce
2 tablespoons flour
½ cup sour cream

Cut the chicken into quarters (if it is whole) and remove the skin and fat. Chop the onions (preferably in a small food processor).

Cook the onions in the butter until they become very soggy. Add more butter if necessary. Blend in 1 tablespoon of the paprika. Stir in the tomato sauce and then add the chicken.

Simmer while covered for one hour, turning the chicken over after ½ hour has passed. Remove the chicken after the one hour has elapsed.

While the chicken is simmering, mix the flour into the sour cream and store it in the refrigerator until the one hour of cooking is completed.

Add the remaining tablespoon of paprika. Add the flour/sour cream mixture to the pot. Simmer, while stirring, for five minutes, or until the mixture becomes well blended and thickened to taste.

Replace the chicken. It may now be stored in the refrigerator. Heat the chicken and sauce together, under low heat, until it is ready to serve.

Before serving, the chicken meat may be taken off the bone and cut into bite size pieces. It goes well with noodles or spätzle, or over biscuits.

This recipe serves four.

Katlyetee

I cannot say that I am completely sure if this spelling is correct. It is a variation of a recipe given to me by an elderly Russian woman (I didn't care for her version – it was too calorific). She told me the name, and I wrote it down as best I could. It is a ground beef dish, easy to make, and can feed a lot of people by simply increasing the ingredients proportionate to the amount of beef used.

Ingredients
1 pound ground beef
large onion, chopped
1 tablespoon dried dill weed
1 ½ teaspoons garlic powder
⅔ stick butter
¼ cup corn starch

In a skillet or pot, melt the butter and sauté the onion. Add the ground beef. Mix it until the beef is completely browned.

Add the dill and garlic powder. Keep stirring until the beef is completely cooked.

Dissolve the corn starch in a small amount of water and add it to the pot. Stir until the desired thickness is achieved.

This dish goes well over rice, mashed potatoes, biscuits, or spätzle.

Shakespeare's Sonnet 29

When in disgrace with fortune and men's eyes,
I all alone beweep my outcast state,
And trouble deaf heaven with my bootless cries,
And look upon myself and curse my fate,
Wishing me like to one more rich in hope,
Featur'd like him, like him with friends possess'd,
Desiring this man's art, and that man's scope,
With what I most enjoy contented least;
Yet in these thoughts myself almost despising,
Haply I think on thee, and then my state,
Like to the lark at break of day arising
From sullen earth, sings hymns at heaven's gate;
For thy sweet love remember'd such wealth brings
That then I scorn to change my state with kings.

Widmung
(Dedication)

Du meine Seele, du mein Herz;

You are my soul, you are my heart;

Du meine Wonn', O du mein Schmerz;

You are my wonder, you are my pain;

Du meine Welt, in der ich lebe;

You are my world, in which I live;

Mein Himmel du, darein ich schwebe;

You are my heaven, wherein I soar;

O du mein Grab,

Oh you my grave,

In das hinab ich ewig meinen Kummer gab!

In which I have eternally laid my griefs!

Du bist die Ruh', und bist der Frieden;

You are rest, and you are peace;

Du bist vom Himmel mir beschieden.

You have departed Heaven for me.

Dass du mich liebst, macht ich mich werth,

That you love me makes me feel worthy,

Dein Blick hat mich vor mir verklärt;

Through your eyes, I see myself more clearly;

Du hebst mich liebend über mich,

Lovingly you lift me out of myself,

Mein guter Geist, mein bess'res Ich!

My good spirit, my better self!

Text by Friedrich Rückert.
Set to music by Robert Schumann.
Translation from the German by the author.

Metaphysics and Ethics

What is metaphysics? The word comes from the Greek for 'beyond physics', which can be taken to mean 'beyond perception and experience'. For our purposes, it can be considered as covering ontology (the study of being), epistemology (the study of knowledge), and cosmology (the study of the universe). Thus, metaphysics could be considered any system of ideas encompassing these things.

In order to see that all people do indeed possess metaphysics, let us take a look at the gamut of systems of ideas that can be shown to fall under these definitions. We should examine each of these things, beginning with ontology, the study of being.

At one extreme is philosophical idealism (which includes the philosophy of Plato and of some Oriental religions). In their ontology, only ideas have genuine reality and matter has only a derivative reality. At the other extreme are the materialists (which must include all of the non-religious). In their ontology, only matter actually exists, and everything else, especially ideas, must be explained in terms of matter. For one who believes in the 'Western' religions, i.e. Christianity, Judaism, or Islam, there is an ontology consisting of a material universe and also a spiritual 'realm', each of which has an actual reality. For those who are concerned only with the existence of what one sees on a day-to-day basis and feel that everything else might as well not exist, that is *their* ontology. Thus, everybody can be said to have some notion of what does exist in reality, and as such, has an ontology.

The next component of metaphysics is epistemology, the study of knowledge, which asks the questions, 'What can we know?', 'What do we know?', and 'How do we know that we know it?'

The philosophical materialists deny the possibility of any knowledge beyond perception and experience, since nothing else connects with the only reality. For them, creativity in ideas is an amalgam of perception and experience. This is akin to considering a recipe as having no flavor beyond its ingredients, and comes close to denying metaphysics itself. Nevertheless, this is their epistemology. There are those, particularly religionists, who claim that there is a non-material entity capable of digesting perception and experience and, from there, creatively producing knowledge that goes beyond these things. This too is an epistemological point of view. There are two interesting dichotomies in epistemology. One exists between those who claim that we can experience reality directly, and those who claim that we can only experience our perception of reality. The other exists between those who claim that there is no limit, other than the effort we put into it, to what we can know, and those who claim that there are limits beyond which our knowledge cannot go. The foregoing represent a very broad range of views, many mutually contradictory, about knowledge. Each view, though, is an epistemology. These views are well thought out, but that is not a requirement. The statement, 'All I know is what they tell me and what I see on TV,' represents an epistemology.

A person's cosmology is not unrelated to his ontology. The basic dichotomy in cosmology is whether or not the universe was created. If it did have a beginning, then there is the question of a 'what' or a 'who' that was the agent of its coming into existence. One school of thought is that there was a creator who ignored the universe after its creation. This is the 'master clockmaker' notion of Isaac Newton and Pierre Simon De La Place. At the opposite pole is the notion of a creator who, after creation, controls every minute aspect of the operation of the universe. This is the view represented by the older religions, particularly in the Hebrew scriptures. It can be called a 'master puppeteer' notion. There is virtually every viewpoint in between, giving rise to a whole spectrum of cosmologies. This spectrum is increased when one takes into account the cosmology which states that the universe has always existed and will always continue to exist. This view, flowing from materialism, of course presupposes no creator. Its proponents invariably consider their view to be 'scientific', while the other is not because it has a way of leading to religion. Yet the hypothesis that the universe had no beginning itself requires a rigorous scientific proof, which is lacking here as much as for the hypothesis of a created universe. It has been my experience that when pressed for their reasons for believing as they do, both sectarian religionists and the non-religious alike form their cosmological views on intuitive 'gut feelings'.

The bottom line of all this is that, while metaphysical systems may vary considerably, everybody has one. It is not a matter of some do and some do not.

What about having an ethics? This can be defined as a set of standards against which a person can determine the good or evil of an act, either before he does it or afterward. These standards can be used to evaluate the good or evil either of one's own acts or the acts of others.

One cannot say that nothing is either good or evil. If that were so, every act would have to be trivial, i.e. any decision as to whether or not to do it could be made purely arbitrarily. More to the point, there would be no need for any agonizing over whether one should *not* do that deed. This is tantamount to saying that every act could be considered good, along with Voltaire's Dr Pangloss, for whom, 'Everything is for the best, in this best of all possible worlds.' I have yet to meet anyone who does not consider the commission of certain acts as worthy of at least public or private scorn or, even more, accountability before the law. (This determination is made by those who theoretically deny good or evil, on the basis of whose ox is being gored. Ironically, the most dogmatic moral absolutes that I have ever heard have come from believers in situational ethics, when it is their ox being gored. For a glossary of terms used in situational ethics, see Appendix E.)

Even those who claim that there is neither good nor evil, consider as evil claiming that such a distinction exists. This type of scorn or demand for accountability implies that there has been a violation of some notion of good or evil and thus lends credence and validity for the existence of such standards. The fact that a person may not always adhere to his ethical standards does not invalidate them. When, in terms of those standards, he does 'good' things, he is following them. When he does 'bad' things, he violates them. The failure to obey one's own ethical code is only a manifestation of human fallibility, and in no way should the code be judged by any violations that are committed against what is taught by it. In this, I have often been asked if my own ethical code has always prevented me from doing something in violation of it. My answer is that it has not, but when I do something wrong, I know that I have done something wrong.

It is easy to see an ethical code in someone who follows a formal doctrine, such as a religious faith or political ideology, no matter how much such a code might vary from one such doctrine to another. In others, it is more subtle yet it can be shown to exist. For the Marxist, who believes in irreconcilable opposites, that which enhances the welfare of the most progressive of these opposites is 'good'. (That the decision as to which side is more progressive rests with Party ideologues, is a side-issue here.) This represents an ethical system. A hedonist also has an ethical code, since anything that enhances his pleasure is good and anything that frustrates it is bad. Likewise, a businessman, whom some would call unscrupulous, who feels that anything that it takes to 'come out on top' or to 'make it sell' is good, has that as his ethical code. Similarly, to a dictator, anything that enhances his power is good, and anything that threatens it is bad.

Thus, as was the case with metaphysics, each person has an ethical system. It cannot be said that some have a moral compass while others do not; it is just that these compasses may point in vastly different directions. Consequently, metaphysical and ethical systems are held by each person, no matter what his point of view, or even if he never stops to think about it. This is true whether these systems were the result of indoctrination or whether they are the result of study and reflection. They are held not only by religionists, but also by atheists and agnostics.

On the topic of indoctrination, it is worth noting that under atheistic Communism people were not encouraged to develop their metaphysics and ethics through study and reflection. Many religious people, on the other hand, have arrived at theirs through these latter methods.

APPENDIX E

Lexicon of Situational Ethics

1. Morally evil: My ox is the one being gored (or the ox belonging to someone I like).

2. Morally good: The ox being gored belongs to someone I don't like.

3. Morally neutral: The ox being gored belongs to people I neither know nor care about.

4. Judging: Holding a poor opinion of me or someone I like.

5. Judgmental: Coming down hard on something I think is not all that bad.

6. Fanaticism: Great enthusiasm for something I disapprove of.

7. Dogmatic: Firm belief in ideas I feel are incorrect.

8. Bad logic: Something that comes to a conclusion that makes me uncomfortable.

9. Demagogue: Someone who makes a convincing case for a viewpoint opposite to my own.

10. Intellectual pride: That defect of character that prevents my adversary from admitting that I am right and he or she is wrong.

11. Irrelevant: An idea or fact that tends to support a position I dislike. (See also: Poor analogy.)

12. Germane: An idea or fact that tends to support a position I like. (See also: Excellent analogy.)

13. Paranoia: Refusal to trust me unquestioningly.

14. Convert: Someone who changes to my beliefs.

15. Apostate: Someone who renounces my beliefs to adopt contrary ones. (See also: Turncoat and renegade.)

16. Loose cannon: Someone who does not subject him or herself to my control.

17. Emotional immaturity: (a) Failing to meet my emotional (and physical) requirements. (b) Holding on to beliefs any possible truth of which escapes me completely.

18. Emotional crutch: Beliefs held by the emotionally immature. (See item 17(b).)

19. Rules are made to be broken: Some rules have a way of getting in the way of my desired lifestyle.

20. Rules must be strictly enforced: Some rules protect the way I like to live.

21. Conservative: A former liberal who's been mugged.

22. Liberal: A former conservative who's been downsized.

23. Forcing others' beliefs on me: When the law requires me to do things I don't like, or refrain from doing things I do like.

24. Promoting responsible behavior: When the law requires others to act in accordance with what I think they should or should not do.

25. Extremist: Views contrary to mine.

26. Moderate: My views.

27. This needs to be discussed further: I'm winning the argument.

28. We should not dwell on the past: I'm losing the argument.

29. Educational: Graphic depictions that support my point of view.

30. Inflammatory: Graphic depictions that undermine my point of view. (See also: Intimidating, Exploitive, Prejudicial, and Inciting.)

31. The will of the people has been thwarted by the small but formidable establishment power structure: My side lost the election.

32. Blasphemy: A criticism of my religious beliefs for which I do not have a credible response at hand.

33. They just don't listen: They won't accept my point of view.

34. Liberty: When I am allowed to do what I like to do.

35. Licence: When people are allowed to do what I think that they shouldn't do.

36. Improvement: Effecting a change from something I do not like to something I do like.

References

1   Sacks, Oliver (9 January 1995) 'Prodigies', *The New Yorker*.

2   Schneider, Edgar (1999) *Discovering My Autism: Apologia Pro Vita Sua (with Apologies to Cardinal Newman)*. London: Jessica Kingsley Publishers.

3   O'Neill, Jasmine Lee (1998) *Through The Eyes Of Aliens*. London: Jessica Kingsley Publishers.

4   I Corinthians 13: 9, 12.

5   Schneider, Edgar: *op. cit.* p.25.

6   Grandin, Temple (1995) *Thinking in Pictures*. New York: Doubleday.

7   Schneider, Edgar: *op. cit.* pp.94–100.

8   Wing, Lorna, Centre for Social and Communication Disorders, London. Private communication, 5 February 1998.

9   Shattock, Paul, University of Sunderland. Private e-mail communication, 29 May 2000.

10   American Psychiatric Association (1994) *Diagnostic and Statistical Manual of Mental Disorders* (4th edn). Washington, DC: American Psychiatric Association.

11   Schneider, Edgar: *op. cit.* pp.96–98.

12   American Psychiatric Association: *op. cit.*

13   American Psychiatric Association: *op. cit.*

14   O'Neill, Jasmine Lee: *op. cit.*

15   Lynn, Shari (1999) *Once a Vegetable, Now a Ham*. Self-published.

16   Schneider, Edgar: *op. cit.* pp.43–45.

17   Martin, Roger, Center for Research, University of Kansas. Review, in *American Scientist* (July–August 2000) of Thomas Lewis, Fari Amini and Richard Lannon (2000) *A General Theory of Love.* New York: Random House.

18   Pascal, Blaise (1623–1662) French mathematician and philosopher.

19   Shaw, George Bernard (1856–1950) From the preface to his play *Getting Married.*

20   Rogers, Richard and Hammerstein, Oscar II (1949) *South Pacific.* New York: Williamson Music.

21   Schneider, Edgar: *op. cit.* p.88.

22   Schneider, Edgar: *op. cit.* p.115.

23   Schneider, Edgar: *op. cit.* pp.90–93.

24   Grandin, Temple: *op. cit.*

25   Engels, Friedrich (1942) *The Origin of the Family, Private Property, and the State.* New York: International Publishers.

26   Cf. Matthew 22: 21.

27   Gray, John (1993) *Men Are From Mars, Women Are From Venus: A Practical Guide for Improving Communication and Getting What You Want In Your Relationships.* New York: HarperCollins.

28   Schneider, Edgar: *op. cit.* p.48.

29   Schneider, Edgar, *op. cit.*

30   Schneider, Edgar: *op. cit.* pp.70–77.

31   Genesis 22: 1–19.

32   John 3: 16.

33   Pushkin, Alexander Sergeyevitch (1799–1837) Russian poet and dramatist.

34   Genesis 1: 27.

35   John 4: 24.

36   *Hamlet*: Act I, Scene 3.

37   Schneider, Edgar: *op. cit.* p.106.

38   Matthew 25: 31–46.

39   Herrnstein, Richard J. and Murray, Charles A. (1994) *The Bell Curve*. New York: Free Press.

40   Churchill, Winston S. (1966) *A History of the English-Speaking Peoples, Volume 2*. New York: Dodd, Mead and Company.

41   Mencken, H.L. and Nathan, George Jean (1948) *An American Credo*. New York: Octagon Books.

42   Schneider, Edgar: *op. cit.* pp.58–60.

43   O'Neill, Jasmine Lee: *op. cit.* p.18.

44   Schneider, Edgar: *op. cit.* pp.11–14.

45   O'Neill, Jasmine Lee: *op. cit.*

46   Schneider, Edgar: *op. cit.* pp.101–105.